Elephants

5.

2/24

ELEPHANTS

Abradale Press

Harry N. Abrams, Inc., Publishers, New York

ELEPH

By Reinhard Künkel

Translated from the German
by Ursula Korneitchouk

H A N T S

Editor, English-language edition: Sheila Steinberg

Library of Congress Cataloging-in-Publication Data
Künkel, Reinhard, 1942–
  [Elefanten. English]
  Elephants / by Reinhard Künkel; translated from the
    German by Ursula Korneitchouk.
    p. cm.
  Translation of: Elefanten.
  ISBN 0–8109–8093–2
  1. African elephant. I. Title.
QL737.P98K8613 1989
599.6′1′096—dc 19   89–418

ACKNOWLEDGMENTS

Most photographs in this volume originated in Tanzania, which boasts an elephant population of more than three hundred thousand—one of the world's largest.

I extend my thanks to the authorities of Tanzania and to the administration of the Tanzania National Parks for giving me the opportunity to take photographs and pursue my research in the country's national parks and wildlife preserves.

I also thank Elias O. Kopulondo, chief park warden of Manyara National Park, for kindly putting a hut of the Musasa Wildlife Observation Post at my disposal, and his gamekeepers and mechanics for their cooperation. I must equally thank David S. Babu, chief park warden of Serengeti National Park, and A. N. G. Mgina, chief curator of Ngorongoro conservation area, for their valuable assistance. I further wish to thank Karl Jähn for much organizational help and useful advice and for putting me up in his camp in the Selous Game Reserve.

While I worked in Tarangire National Park, I was lodged in the Tarangire Tent Camp. I thank its manager and staff for their hospitality and practical help, in particular Chimanbhai Patel, who, as he had in the past, always proved ready to help when I approached him with my numerous organizational problems; his resourcefulness turned the Tarangire office into an important base.

Once again, I am indebted to my friends at Ndutu Lodge for countless favors and aid. I need only mention Tom-Tom, as representative of the whole crew. Tirelessly and with a patient smile he kept mending my thorn-punctured tires, sometimes three or four a day.

I also want to thank Harvey Croze for information and hints and for an interesting dinner conversation on the subject of elephants.

Last, not least, it is high time that I thank Barbie Allen in Nairobi, on whose help and advice I have depended for years and whose support has contributed greatly to the success of my work.

To Inge Pothier, who typed almost half the manuscript and peeled the mangoes—*merci*!

Reinhard Künkel
Watamu, Kenya
March 1981

CONTENTS

PREFACE

Elephants exude superb calm and dignity. This is, admittedly, a personal view and one not often accepted as a universal truth. Undeniably, elephants—our companions through time and evolution—are unique and fascinating creatures. But too few people have appreciated them in these terms, and far too many see them only as sources of ivory and dog food, which requires their slaughter, or as competitors for the earth's food and space, which justifies it. Year after year, some fifty to one hundred fifty thousand of these peaceable giants are butchered for their tusks, and thousands more are killed for food or simply for being where people wish to be. The pressures of our bulging population are making us ever more dangerous and cruel neighbors.

In the meanest utilitarian sense, living elephants are, in truth, not "useful." In fact, they can be hard on their environment—though arguably not nearly so hard as we. They destroy trees, turning forests into savannahs, and where planted fields lie across their paths they may traipse over them with lordly unconcern. Even on the immense African continent, with its human inhabitants daily increasing, such depredations are coming to seem unaffordable. The fate of the elephants, caught between the human population explosion and the ivory trade as between the closing blades of giant shears, looks bleak.

Is there anything to be said in favor of elephants? A great deal! I have attempted to capture and convey in this book at least a few facets of their lives and to plead, with my photographs and sketches of their behavior, for the future of these behemoths who are at once so mighty and so defenseless, so "useless" and so utterly lovable.

AFRICAN MORNING

The rising sun hovered above a dead tree, its blaze seeming to singe the wing tips of two crested cranes who were late in leaving their sleeping place. On the lake, pelicans fluttered clumsily to their fishing grounds. Some impala rams strolled along the shore. Reflected in the shimmering water, their slender shapes lost all color and weight and became graceful silhouettes stalking through liquid silver. A hippopotamus bull emerged from the bushes. Announcing his coming with one high- and five low-pitched trumpet blasts, he lumbered across the sand, splashed into the water, and disappeared into a group of dark hippopotamus backs that rose from the waves a hundred yards offshore. The hippos would spend the day dozing in the water; only at dark would they return to land to graze.

I sat on the roof of my Land-Rover enjoying the cool air and soft light, letting my field glasses sweep across the African landscape. The steep sides of the rift valley rise, in places, twenty-six hundred feet above Lake Manyara, and to these heights the elephants had climbed during the night. Soon I picked out one group wandering along a winding ridge; a little below, a second group was descending a steep path. The clear morning promised a hot day, and the elephants were leaving their nocturnal pastures early enough to reach the acacia forests and watering places before the heat became intense. On cool, rainy days, by contrast, it might be noon before they returned to the plain. Their swaying movements, trunks swinging like pendulums, kept them in balance on the precipitous terrain. Their heads bobbed to the rhythm of their steps, making their ears flap around their shoulders like the sails of becalmed ships. Despite the difficult and dangerous descent, the animals seemed completely relaxed, often stopping to pluck grass and leaves. A young bull playfully snatched a long branch and chewed on its tip. Only one cow with a calf in tow was restless and aggressive. With a violent swing of her tusks, she shoved aside an adolescent bull who had probably come too close; he briefly lost his footing and slipped a few yards downhill.

The elephants roamed the steep slopes like colossal mountain goats, repeatedly interrupting their descent to eat at length. They plucked bushes to shreds, dug for roots, and broke large branches from the few trees that had taken root at those heights. On reaching gentler slopes, they halted briefly under a baobab, perhaps to rest or to reconnoiter the land below—then abruptly took off again at a lively pace, as if in sudden haste to reach the acacia forests, which finally swallowed them up in a jumble of trunks, branches, fallen trees, and shifting shadow and light.

A few hours later, sitting under a tree, I was treated to an arresting spectacle: A herd of about eighty elephants was passing in a broad front through the acacia grove. The wind was favorable so that the elephants couldn't pick up my scent. They approached, grew larger, became gigantic, and finally were so close that I could hear the sand crunch under their soft, flat feet. One contingent slipped past my hiding place at a distance of barely twenty yards. The silence of their drifting passage was astounding until they came to a deeply cut riverbed that lay across the path to their watering place. There, two of the calves immediately plopped into the sand and slid down on their bellies. They burrowed their trunks playfully into the soft ground and spewed trunkloads of dust on each other's backs. Then they ran exuberantly through the dry bed, each step powdering the air with a jet of sand. The herd had almost disappeared into the brush on the opposite bank before these two abandoned their game and hurried to join their elders, who were placidly swaying through the bush.

FLIGHT

I was driving along a bumpy track that led down to the river. The valley lay in shadow, apparently empty, and tree trunks and underbrush blocked my view. I drove around a bend and there, suddenly, were elephants—not many but very large. As startled as I was, I brought the car to a skidding, squealing, dust-billowing halt, but the elephants were not mollified. Angry trumpet signals shrilled through the thicket, accompanied by energetic flapping of ears and indignant shaking of heads. The underbrush splintered under the stomping. I withdrew as fast as I could, in part for my own safety and also because I hoped by retreating to restore their tranquility.

But there was no quieting them. My abrupt and unexpected arrival had plunged them into panic. From a small elevation that offered a view of the valley I discovered that the fellows I had disturbed were but the small advance guard of a struggling herd of about one hundred, among which the panic began to spread like brushfire. Their trumpeting, at once frightened and furious, swelled to an apocalyptic chorus that shattered the forlorn stillness of the morning. A hundred elephants roared through the valley. Branches snapped, saplings toppled, impenetrable undergrowth was trampled flat. A cloud of dust rose into the air like an ominous distress signal—a fog that enveloped the herd in ghostly light. At moments, I could distinguish the shape of a calf among the racing giants, anxiously trying to keep up with its mother.

The elephants kept running, fleeing headlong in blind terror, urging one another on with piercing cries of alarm. A half hour after the spate of bodies, the gray dust, the strident din had finally been swallowed up around a river bend, I still heard occasional trumpet blasts in the far distance. Never had I

13

seen elephants run so fast, so far.

At first, I had watched the stampede in a daze. Then I reproached myself for my awkwardness, which, I thought, had put the herd into headlong flight. But later, when I told the story to one of the gamekeepers, he had a different, more plausible explanation: Elephants, being oblivious to the boundaries of their parks and preserves, sometimes wander through neighboring territories, where angry farmers fearing for their crops fire warning shots to drive them away and where poachers shoot to kill. The herd I encountered may well have had some bitter experience not long before, and that would account for their seemingly inordinate terror.

VALOR AND DISCRETION

On the plain by the lake was a spot where the ground lay bare. The elephants often came here to dig and eat the salt- and mineral-rich earth. They loosened the crusted soil with the hard toe-rims of their front feet, then shoved the chunks into their mouths with their trunks. Some cows, wanting more than they could loosen with their feet, went down on their knees to break up the earth with their tusks. Some of the younger animals also knelt down, trying to pick up the salt-rich substance directly with their mouths. The animals' craving for salt was obviously stronger even than mother love: The calves, trying continually to snatch some salt earth from their mothers, were invariably pushed aside.

The salt lick was much in demand; one group after another made for the shallow pit in the course of a morning. Since the salt lick could accommodate only one family unit at a time, impatient newcomers might attempt to drive the present occupants off. But a certain hierarchy among the lead cows seemed clearly to apply: If the approaching group was headed by a matriarch of higher rank, the current tenants would retreat at the first, often barely hinted threat; it follows that lower-ranking newcomers had to wait until their predecessors chose to leave.

Normally, the dissolved salt in the elephants' drinking water suffices to meet their need. They prefer water with a high concentration of minerals and sometimes undertake long treks to reach such watering places. Lacking these, they will dig up the soil around natural salt licks; sometimes they even break up whole termite hills, which are as hard as concrete, simply to get at the enriched soil of these insect citadels. In the Ngorongoro conservation area there is a rock face with a cave deep enough comfortably to hold a fully grown, standing bull elephant. Tusk imprints reminiscent of chisel marks crisscross its walls and ceiling. These must have taken the elephants, in their search for salt, decades—even centuries—to carve.

One morning I came upon an assembly of about eighty elephants in the vicinity of the salt lick, with five or six hundred buffalo grazing nearby. Two hours later, prompted by the growing heat, the elephants decamped for a mud bath to the only wallow of the region, closely followed by the buffalo. A silent phalanx of the latter surrounded the bathing elephants at a distance of about fifty yards. A few especially impatient buffalo bulls ventured closer, but about ten yards away they stopped in their tracks, stared motionlessly at the elephants for several minutes, suddenly shook their heads, and seconds later resumed their transfixed staring.

After their mud bath, the elephants moved to the nearby

salt lick. The buffalo followed in short order and surrounded them again. Gradually both herds streamed out onto the plain, the small groups of elephants looking like gray islands emerging from a sea of buffalo backs. The older elephants suffered the buffalos' impertinent proximity with equanimity, but an occasional juvenile tried to chase the intruders with threats and mock attacks. An enraged four- or five-year-old charged one buffalo who had ventured far too close, but when the offender didn't budge but only stared mistrustfully at his attacker, the young elephant, visibly chastened by such colossal fearlessness, hesitated briefly, then wheeled around and hurried back to the safety of his family. A more mature male, already endowed with arm-long tusks and a most impressive bulk, had better luck. His thrust, accompanied by irate trumpeting, drove his opponent back, if only ten or twenty yards.

Another time, I saw the lead cow of an elephant group rout an enormous buffalo from the wallow where he had dozed through the afternoon. On the whole, however, only young elephants will attack other animals, either in play or because they want to show off and are looking for a victim. I once observed a pubescent male stomping up and down a riverbed in seemingly violent rage, then, warrior and trumpeter in one, charging two warthogs whose only offense was to be nearby digging for roots. Tails pointing skyward, the hogs escaped. In need of a new target, the young challenger then turned against six zebras grazing on the other side of the riverbed. Having frightened them into a brief canter, he crowned his efforts by scaring off some vultures that had been sitting on the bank, wings outstretched to dry after their morning ablutions. The rest of his troop ignored their impetuous comrade's exploits, browsing peacefully the while. Some days later, as the same elephants were passing a group of baboons, one of the calves suddenly veered, ears flapping, and rushed the startled primates, who escaped up the nearest tree, whence they railed at the troublemaker at the top of their voices. Impalas too, who frequently browse near elephants, occasionally become targets of their adolescent exuberance, to which they generally respond with what seems appropriate nonchalance.

Despite their size, elephants by no means claim undisputed precedence in all their dealings with other animals. The privileges they might derive from their awesomeness and strength they are often too gentle and peaceable to claim. An elephant family, including an enormous bull, was resting by the edge of a pool, eyes shut, drowsing away the afternoon. Two crested cranes came stalking up in leisurely search of food. On reaching the water, they first quenched their thirst, then began prancing around each other with outspread wings. At the first steps of their mating dance the elephants rose abruptly and, to escape the annoying commotion, took off without a sound.

Normally, rhinoceroses spend daylight hours in the water, coming to shore to feed only at night. But one afternoon, on the plain by the Musasa River, a rhinoceros strayed into a herd of elephants. One of the bulls headed menacingly for the myopic leviathan but lost heart after a few steps and beat a retreat, and the rest of the herd hurriedly opened a zigzag path for the waddling, agitated rhino. When, very early the next morning, another rhino emerged from the thicket and headed slowly toward the river, browsing as he came, the feeding elephants gradually grew so disquieted at his approach that they crossed uneasily to the other bank.

A similar episode that unfolded in the Selous area likewise illustrates the somewhat mistrustful coexistence of hippos and elephants. Four elephants ambled along the shore of the Rufiji River where it fans out into several channels, finally finding a convenient ford. They slowly waded into the loamy current up to their bellies, then to their shoulders. A few more steps, and the animals had to swim. Only the tops of their heads and their eyes protruded above the water, and the tips of their trunks poked through the river surface like the periscopes of a squadron of submarines. They crossed the water single file, soon regained their footing, and one by one emerged to their full height on the opposite shore, their wet bulks gleaming darkly. Across a narrow strip of sand lay the next arm of the river, which they also had to ford to reach the juicy reed fields of the bog beyond, but in the very center of this stream a tight cluster of thirty or forty hippos formed a living island. One of the hippos, perturbed by the sudden appearance of the elephants, raised his head and blared a sequence of ominous bass tones into the quiet morning. The elephants flapped their ears, raised their trunks, spun around, and ran off in the direction from which they had just come. In their unseemly haste, they resembled agitated fat men whose suspenders have broken and who are struggling to keep up their speed, their dignity, and their trousers. The waters seethed and foamed as they crashed once more into the flood. Back on the far shore, they rested from the excitement and exertion of two crossings. A full half hour later they made a fresh start, but this time they walked about a hundred yards upstream to avoid the hippos, and only then crossed both channels to the longed-for reed fields.

TOPPLING TREES

The biggest of the six bulls, standing at least twelve feet high, headed for an acacia tree with a broad umbrella-like canopy. When he reached the tree, he stopped and craned his neck, and his trunk shot up to the tangle of branches like the telescopic ladder of a fire truck. He had to stretch mightily, even to stand a-tiptoe (so to speak) on his right foot, to bridge the last inches to a branch whose lowest tips he finally managed to grab with his two trunk fingers. He tugged at the branch, screwed the tip of his trunk around the twigs to get a better hold, pulled a little more, wound his trunk a second time around the foliage—much like winding a dog leash around one's wrist—and, then firmly gripping the boughs he had twisted into a rope, pulled with all his strength. The rope resisted only for seconds; then a portion of the treetop came noisily crashing down.

The elephants immediately threw themselves upon the fresh greens. In no time the torn branches were stripped nearly clean, and the lead bull reached for the treetop again. His first try fell short, and he lowered his trunk in preparation for a more strenuous tactic. Clutching the fork of a branch with the tip of his raised trunk, he took the tree trunk between his tusks and pressed his forehead against it with such force that the whole tree began to sway. The elephant pushed, stepped back, pushed again, three, four times. With each assault, the bull bent the tree a little farther before allowing it to swing back. After the fifth push, it swung back no more but arched in slow motion to the ground. The crash shattered the afternoon quiet for miles around. Three more elephants left the tree on which they had been feeding a few hundred yards off to share in the new feast.

For the next hour the elephants were busy, tearing the tree-top apart with their trunks, tusks, and forefeet, and chewing it up. Only rarely was there some minor trouble, when a low-ranking elephant plucked the choicest greens from under the nose of a higher-up, in which case the stronger animal simply shoved the weaker one aside, causing a chain reaction of rearrangements in the feeding order. But once or twice such an altercation led to serious confrontation, and then the higher-ranking elephant dealt his rival a blow with his heavy tusks that made their relative ranks and prerogatives unmistakably clear.

In 1978 the acacia forest around Lake Legaja and Lake Masak saw an invasion of perhaps fifty bulls. These two small soda lakes in southwestern Serengeti form the beginning of the famous Olduvai Gorge, only some twenty to twenty-five miles from Laetoli, an excavation site that yielded, among other things, the fossilized footprints of prehistoric proboscideans. Under normal conditions, elephants seldom stray into this dry area; but there had been two unusually good rainy seasons, and the water of the swollen lakes may well have attracted the animals. In the succeeding dry period, however, little food was available besides the leaves and twigs of the umbrella acacias, and two months after the "invasion" of the elephants, whole stretches of woodland looked as if an armored brigade had held war games there. Trees were broken and toppled everywhere, strewn pell-mell across the landscape, and the silence was uncanny, almost oppressive.

The fifty bulls were divided into several gangs. As a rule, only males form the advance guard that scouts new territory; the cows and their young follow later. I once observed such a tree-felling squad for several days. On the first day, the bulls toppled five trees, on the second day six, and another six on the third. They didn't even take turns at the job; almost all trees were felled by the same bull. Unfortunately I couldn't follow them after dark, for I would have gotten hopelessly stuck in the tangle of fallen trees; and, also, although elephants do sleep for a few hours after midnight, they spend a large part of their nights searching for food. (Actually, up to eighteen of every twenty-four hours are spent gathering fresh greens.) "My" group must surely have felled some additional trees at night.

Such prowess can uproot an astonishing number of trees. Peter Guy estimates that elephants in the Sengwa region of Zimbabwe toppled

56,000 trees each year within an area of about 385 square miles. This alarming figure, however, constitutes a mere one percent of the trees within the area.

Even trees too huge to be uprooted often fall victim to the elephants, hollowed out or girdled by their tusks. In Tarangire National Park, there is hardly a baobab without a broad ring of bark scraped off by elephant tusks. This species of tree also has a particularly soft, fibrous wood that the elephants like to dig out, sometimes gouging veritable caves in these bizarre plant-mountains, so that the trees eventually collapse under their own weight. In Tarangire a few years ago, in a stroke of grisly irony, an elephant was killed, his spine broken by the weight of a collapsing baobab.

MIDDAY BATHS

At noontime, "my" group regularly went down to their watering place at the shore of Lake Masak. After drinking, they waded into deeper water to enjoy a lengthy bath. The weighty creatures slid under the water; bobbed up again; rolled from side to side, raising their trunks like periscopes above the surface to draw in several cubic yards of air; and slowly submerged again. Reappearing, they shoved and jostled in play and friendly combat, mounting each other, ramming one another with their tusks, rolling over to yield to their opponents' thrust, pushing each other's heads under the water, and reemerging to snort the air, only to disappear again in the lake. Their trunks writhed like the tentacles of giant octopuses, sometimes getting tangled into knots, and their tusks glistened like walrus fangs among the waves. When they exhaled below the water, little geysers suddenly bubbled on the surface. One bull, his flapping ears whipping up a small storm, trumpeted at a tiny diver bird that wanted to fish in the murky flood under the elephant's nose; for the agitated waters promised a plentiful catch of fish that day.

From my hiding place in the bushes I had observed the bulls enjoying their bathing for quite a while. As the animals lumbered still farther out into the lake, I was suddenly seized by the spirit of adventure. I yearned to swim with the elephants. Dumping my clothes into the car, I snatched a camera and one of the lighter telephoto lenses and plunged in the water. My lark very quickly turned into strenuous work: I had to keep the camera dry, and that left me with only one arm and two legs for swimming. To get close to the elephants, I had to swim about seventy yards—admittedly a modest stretch, but one that, with the weight of the camera, seemed considerable. The closer I came to the splashing behemoths, the more the camera weighed me down. Only a few more yards. My lungs burned as I tried to catch my breath. I forced myself on—for should I drown, I wanted to leave these pictures.

I somehow managed the last few yards that brought the animals within my camera range. But the toughest part was yet to come: I had to tread water with exhausted legs while using both hands to adjust the camera. Finally the water appeared more or less horizontally in the viewfinder. The elephants swam past the focused lens. The picture looked sharp. The animals seemed excitingly near. I pushed the button—two, three times—then I gave up. I couldn't move my legs; my arms felt leaden. I had to lie back to catch my breath. The elephants, ten or twelve yards off, didn't take unfair advantage and try to sink me and my equipment. Though they occasionally glanced at me, they seemed to take me for one of the puffed-up ducks cruising nearby. Luckily, a dead tree was sticking out of the water not too far away. I found a fork in it for my camera and, feeling tons lighter, clung to it for a few moments. The elephants continued to romp in the water with noisy delight.

After a brief rest, I felt mysteriously drawn to them and wanted to experience them at closest range. Leaving my camera behind, I was able to use both arms to swim toward them. I felt much stronger. Ten more yards, eight, seven—then, suddenly, the elephants noticed me. Like cobras obeying a snake charmer's tune, their trunks came out of the water. But as I had approached against the wind, they couldn't pick up my scent. I held still until they retracted their probing truks. Perhaps they took me for another big duck, or even a goose. Slowly, cautiously, I pushed closer. I felt elated. Her I was, swimming with the wild elephants, almost close enough to touch them. I lost all fear and felt so free I thought I could fly. At the same time I was keenly alert and watched the animals' every move. Without a sound, I slid another yard closer. The bulls rolled phlegmatically along. Suddenly, the elephant next to me raised his head and stared at me. Then he thrust his trunk out of the water to suck in some air. His probing eyes kept searching. He seemed vaguely displeased. The splashing stopped abruptly. The other bulls eyed me mistrustfully. I found myself nearly encircled by the now-silent creatures. The elephant in front of me seemed to ponder whether his trunk would be long enough to grab me and hold me underwater. I didn't wait for his decision. Slowly, and as quietly as possible, I backed away, keeping a careful eye on the bull. Gaining yard by yard, I finally put a safe distance between me and the elephants. Feeling weak in the knees, I swam to the dead tree, pcked up my camera, and pushed back to the shore. I was damned glad when I reached firm ground.

FATAL WOUNDS

Only the biggest and strongest bulls fell trees. Cows, on the other hand, use a totally different method to attack them, but one that in the long run is equally devastating.

A cow and two calves, one four and the other perhaps eight years old, were standing under an acacia tree. Using one tusk as a lever, the mother pried a strip of bark loose until it was long enough for her to grip it firmly with her trunk. Then, pulling steadily, she peeled off a layer about two yards long. The two youngsters worked in similar fashion, trying hard to rip off some of the tough strips. But they lacked strength, and their tusks were too short to inflict more than a few small scratches upon the tree. Still, they were learning to imitate their mother and to appreciate the taste of bark. When the threesome strolled off two hours later, they left behind a fatally wounded tree. Although the rainy season had already begun and vegetation abounded, elephants were attacking increasingly large numbers of trees. At this time of year, at least, the fibrous strips of bast seemed to be a juicy addition to the elephants' regular diet, although quantitatively they added up to less nourishment than the three animals could have gathered within the same two hours had they eaten grass and foliage. The elephants seemed to peel bark mainly during the hot midday hours, which they prefer to spend in the shadow of trees anyway. Perhaps they were bored. Or perhaps they found bark a handy substitute for grass and greenery while the blazing sun kept them from grazing.

Four days after I first saw a cow stripping an acacia, I met another group of cows and calves spending their siesta under a large tree. While the others dozed, the lead cow busily peeled off long ribbons of bark. Filaments of bast had been ripped off the wood all the way up to a main fork in the trunk, and two- and three-yard-long strips were dangling above the elephants like ropes from the mast of a ship. After a while, the cow lost interest and all the animals began to wander off. Only a young bull remained. He fished for the bark, clutched the end of a strip, pulled, lost his grip, reached up again, playfully set the jumble of bast strips swinging all at once like bell-ropes, and then, pulling

24

one strip far enough down to catch it between his teeth, sunk to his knees to tear it off with his weight. The tough fiber resisted. Undaunted, the bull began to pull a second time. Again he slipped off. The ardent tug-of-war went on for ten to fifteen minutes. Despite his clumsy bulk, the young bull in his exuberance reminded me of an oversized cat clawing for threads of yarn.

Unfortunately, such sport has the direst consequences for the forest, directed as it is against one kind of acacia while sparing the others. In Manyara National Park, for instance, elephants single out the *Acacia tortilis*, killing more than five percent of these trees each year. In places the acacia forest resembles a bizarre sculpture garden in which skeletons lift their bleached branches skyward in silent accusation. Why elephants inflict such damage on trees is not yet understood. Some researchers suspect that the calcium-rich bark helps them meet a nutritional requirement; others think that the sap attracts elephants as irresistibly as honey attracts bears.

Elephants are surprisingly versatile and inventive. While they can doom a tree by attacking the top, or by stripping the bark, or simply by felling it, some pachyderms prefer to get at the root of the matter. One noontime, I came across a cow patiently digging out a massive rootstock. Her left tusk was missing (possibly lost in a similar endeavor), but she used her right tusk as a gigantic weapon to ferret out the recalcitrant root—at first without success. She persisted. Having kicked the surrounding earth loose, she seized the stock with her trunk, slipped her tusk underneath it as a lever, and pried as hard as she could. The wood groaned, but held firm. The cow repeatedly kicked the root with the front edge of her front foot, then angled and squeezed the foot underneath it and pressed forward. The wood creaked from the strain, but still didn't splinter apart. Next she placed the same foot on the other side of the root and drew it toward her. Again, the wood moaned. Again, she attacked with her tusk. A piece of root was laid bare; she kicked the earth loose at both ends of it. After twenty minutes of relentless exertion, she jerked the root from its anchorage. Holding its free end between her teeth, she removed the tough outer skin with her trunk. Having peeled the choicest part like a banana and devouring it, she carelessly discarded the rest.

SUPERIOR FORCES

The sun had climbed halfway up the eastern sky. It was still early in the day, but a group of elephants had already gathered by the river and were drawing up water in long drafts in their trunks to quench their thirst. Then they ambled one by one over to an enormous tree whose foliage formed so vast a roof that all twenty-eight giants could rest in the shade beneath. A tribe of green monkeys frolicked in the sweeping branches, swinging down from their tails and ranting and raving at the uninvited guests below. They barked and twanged and hollered in every possible pitch, according to their size. Suddenly, the pachyderms, too, were growling and trumpeting. The squad got up, circled furiously once around the tree, then calmed down again. What had disturbed them was a second group of elephants passing by, a short distance away, on their way to the water. The monkeys kept railing, but without the slightest effect on the elephants.

Some calves were sleeping between the legs of the adults, their breath whipping up the dust at the end of their trunks. One of the cows found a crooked stick, about two yards long, which kept her occupied for quite a while. She placed it across her tusks, raised it over her back, and swung it around with such abandon that she finally knocked a calf over the head with it. The calf grabbed the stick and pulled as hard as he could, but was no match for the cow and quickly lost the tug-of-war. Then the cow dropped her toy, picked it up again, dangled it over her back, threw it aside, and picked it up a second time after a short interval. And so it went, until she discovered by accident that the crooked stick fit precisely under her chin. As if resting her head on a pillar, she leaned on the stick, holding this position for two or three minutes before finally dropping the stick and proceeding to massage one of her earlobes with her trunk.

On another occasion an elephant cow was standing next to me, eyes closed, head similarly propped on a forked branch. She remained in this position for a full ten minutes. Young elephants, too, enjoy playing at length with all sorts of sticks, from the flexible twigs of shrubbery to tree branches almost too heavy for them to lift. The elephant's pleasure in manipulating large and heavy bulk material has been put to good use for centuries, particularly in Asia, where elephants used to serve—and in a few places still do—as living cranes in lumberyards.

Soon the herd left their resting place and trotted southward through luminous woodlands. After a lengthy march, the lead cow guided them to a pool replenished during a thunderstorm three days earlier. Two Nile geese had alighted at the edge of the pool, but quickly retreated with much clucking and wing beating, yielding to the superior force of the gray colossuses. As the elephants had already had their bath for the day, only their young rolled briefly in the wallow; the older animals continued on their way after taking perhaps a shower or two with their trunks. Some stragglers in the herd met the two Nile geese again, who were waddling back to the pool to reclaim their territory after the passage of this mammoth force to be reckoned with.

27

AT THE LAKE

The noon heat weighed on the lake like liquid glass. Soundlessly, the sun hammered its rays into the sand. Five bull elephants, sand crunching under their steps, approached the shore, used their trunks and front feet to dig hollows into the soft ground, and then waited patiently for water to collect in the wells. The leisurely drinking process took one, perhaps even two hours. At long last, they waded knee-high into the lake. There they stopped and stood for a long time, dozing as the shallow waves lapped around their legs. After a while, the coolness of the water revived their playful spirits. Two bulls suddenly intertwined their trunks, locked tusks, and tried to push each other aside. The water splashed high around them, covering their bodies with a dark, wet, glistening veneer.

This water battle was too good to miss, so I drove as close to it as possible on the sandy shore. One bull resented the disturbance. Without warning, he came rushing at me through the flood, ears spread like the sails of a frigate, pushing a huge bow wave before him. I stood still. Enveloped in foam, he reached shore barely ten yards from my car—and then skipped around. After pacing nervously back and forth and jerking his erect head angrily at me, he withdrew, his spectacular attack petering out by the water hole he had dug a short time earlier. Unimpressed by their comrade's fierce sally, the other bulls strolled stolidly back to shore. Another stop at their drinking places, and they disappeared into the tall shrubs surrounding the sandy shore.

A few days later, in the same area, I met a lone bull weighed down by an enormous pair of tusks. He was loafing through the afternoon, plucking a tuft of grass here, a few leaves from a shrub there. Then under a tree he found some fruits that were obviously his favorites, for he thoroughly scanned the ground under the branches. He didn't find too many of the olive green, plum-sized delicacies; other elephants before him had already conducted a similar search. But he had a solution: He took the tree trunk between his tusks and shook it. Plums rained down. With great deliberation, he collected his harvest, groping along the ground with his trunk until he found a fruit, taking it between his two trunk fingers, and shoving it into his mouth. The tip of his trunk shuttled steadily between ground and mouth. Often, with a flick of his trunk fingers, he would flip a fruit into his gullet from about ten inches' distance, a time-saving trick he mastered like a pro, for I must have watched him do it flawlessly a hundred times. It took him a half hour to gather the crop. Then he shook a second glut of fruits from the tree. This time he merely picked another dozen or two and lazily went his way.

ORDER AND LAW

Elephants live in a matriarchal society. Iain Douglas-Hamilton studied the herds in Manyara National Park for several years and found that cow/calf groups, comprising several mature cows and their young of all ages, form the core of elephant society. A lead cow heads each group, and several such groups form a larger federation in which all members are bonded by varying degrees of blood relationship. As females usually spend their lifetime within a kinship unit, these groups often span three generations.

Because of the elephant's huge demand for food—depending on its size, an adult animal digests two to five hundred pounds of greenery daily—families are constantly roaming the land. In the process, they adapt marvelously to local conditions. With the exception of desert regions, every kind of environment throughout Africa is inhabited by elephants. Despite their bulk, our largest land animals even turn up on the slopes of Mount Kilimanjaro and Mount Kenya, at heights well above thirteen hundred feet; yet on rare occasions, they can also be found at sea level, near the Indian Ocean for instance.

Water also determines where the herds wander; the animals need to drink at least once a day, and they consume one hundred or more quarts of water at a time. During the several months of the rainy season, their whole existence revolves around water holes, whence they strike out at any time of day or night on long treks in search of food, only to return within twenty-four hours to their watering place.

Their food consists mainly of every kind of plant foliage, but they are quite capable of living almost exclusively on grass for long periods if little else is available. Their need for food is so great that they can hardly afford to be choosy; yet they do show distinct preferences for specific kinds of plants or fruit. The intoxicating palm fruit, for example, is a favorite. Bananas are another. It isn't hard to imagine the ravages a herd of elephants can inflict on a banana or corn plantation. Formerly, when the natives saw their fields threatened by elephants, they did what they could to scare them off with noise and tam-tams. Later, farmers tried to spoil the robbers' appetite for the forbidden fruit by peppering their behinds with buckshot. Several years ago, in Kenya, when a herd of more than one hundred elephants advanced from the dry northeastern prairies toward the farm belt of the adjacent highlands, the defenders of this agricultural Garden of Eden used helicopters to crack down on the pachyderms, driving them off their lucrative high-yield paradise with vicious, low-level attacks. For several decades, elephants have simply been—and still are—gunned down by professional sharpshooters.

When puberty sets in, the twelve- to fifteen-year-old bulls are expelled from the matriarchal groups by the females. For a while they follow at a distance, then they join the other bulls. Only when fully grown will they again visit the matriarchs' herds on occasion to mate with the cows. Thereafter, whether or not the mating was successful, the bulls go their own way again.

In times of scarcity or stress, many elephant groups band together to form larger herds; no doubt the animals feel more secure in a big herd when fleeing from hunters or after a lead cow has been gunned down. Defending themselves against humans or other predators, they will often put up a united front. One of nature's rarest and most impressive spectacles is a tightly packed wall of elephants—heads high, tusks shining like rows of spears ready for combat.

Elephants show no territorial instinct. Ranges overlap without causing the least tension between groups. Ranges also vary greatly in size, depending on geographical conditions and the availability of food and water. In Manyara National Park, with its rich vegetation and plentiful water supply, the average range of an elephant group encompasses less than twenty square miles; but in the western part of Tsavo National Park, an average range measures more than one hundred forty square miles, and in the dry eastern region of the park a range may cover six hundred forty square miles.

PROCREATION

A peacefully grazing elephant herd spread out across the sun-drenched plain. Abruptly, two huge bulls charged each other. An angry trumpet call announced the battle. Tusks clashed, trunks tangled like wrestling pythons as the elephants tried to push each other aside. Twisting their heads, they shoved and pressed, punched each other with their tusks, disentangled themselves, stared at each other for a second, motionless, then charged again with the ferocity of a cyclops. Each tried to use his trunk to steady his opponent for the next thrust. Though both animals were roughly the same size, the match quickly proved unequal. The weaker rival yielded more and more frequently, gradually losing ground. The intervals between attacks grew longer. After another duel, the weaker of the two heavyweights not only stepped aside, but had to withdraw altogether to catch his breath. Then he again charged his opponent, a gigantic six-tonner, was shoved around, and surrendered by simply turning around and walking off. The victor pursued him for a few paces, but changed his mind and stopped to pluck a bunch of grass instead.

The oft-interrupted fight had lasted barely a half hour. Both animals came away unscratched. Confrontations among bulls—generally a simple matter of rank—usually end without bloodshed. They occur quite frequently among younger males, who must compete for privileged positions and subsequently must keep defending these. But among mature bulls fights are rare. I therefore suspected that the violence I had witnessed had something to do with the cows, or, more precisely, with their readiness to mate.

Cows remain in heat for three weeks, but they can conceive for only three days. While in heat, they mate with a number of bulls. Actual copulation is a matter of less than a minute.

Two days later, my guess was confirmed. Several elephant families were grazing along the lake shoreline near the acacia forest. The victor of the earlier duel was passing among the cows, testing their willingness to mate by touching their genitals with his trunk. Cows are seldom in a responsive mood; most of the time they simply ignore male advances. But this time, the gray giant detected positive signs in one cow. He was beside himself with excitement, shook his head, trumpeted, and went so impetuously after the cow that she retreated hastily. But not too far. Less than one hundred yards away she allowed the impassioned bull to catch up to her, put his trunk around her, and mount her.

The awesome primeval act of procreation triggered a second, equally dramatic spectacle. Excited, the other elephants ran up to the couple, pressed around, and filled the air with a blaring serenade of shrill dissonance, all the while bumping their heads and twisting their trunks into strange configurations. Startled calves ran around amid the confusion, helplessly waiting for the riotous pageant to end. And at the center of the commotion, almost motionless, stood the bull and the cow.

Elephants have the longest gestation period of any animal—twenty to twenty-two months. The cow I had seen copulate was easy to identify by the notches in her ear. I had taken a picture of her at the time of the mating and nearly two years later was determined to find her again. It was a long search. For four weeks I looked for her in vain. Then, one afternoon in the Endabash area, I found her. I recognized her at once and was greatly relieved, for I had begun to fear that she might have been killed by poachers or otherwise have met an untimely death. At the same time, however, I had a bitter disappointment. The calf I had hoped to find was nowhere to be seen. Nor did the cow show any sign of motherhood, such as swollen mammaries. The mating had not resulted in pregnancy, and I had to shelve my plans to photograph mother and infant.

NEW TO THE BUSH

I was driving my car slowly, heading for the edge of a pool where I had noticed a prairie eagle and an African sea eagle who seemed to be fighting over some prey. My Land-Rover bumped into a hole, shrieked, and stopped. The two frightened birds flew off, leaving behind a few large shreds of skin. When I was at last close enough to examine the dark bundle, I realized that I had made an interesting discovery: An elephant cow had dropped her afterbirth here; she must have given birth recently somewhere in the vicinity. As only the two eagles had spotted the embryonic sack, she could have discharged it merely a short time before. The cow and her newborn couldn't be far. I had to find them.

Tall grass and thick brush slowed me down. I stopped frequently to climb onto the roof of my car in order to survey the surroundings through my binoculars, but I could see only a few impalas and eventually two warthogs scurrying through the thicket. I drove a wide half circle around the area where I thought the herd might be. After a long period of forcing my way through the dense bush, I suddenly saw the gray backs of animals in front of me. I cautiously crept closer.

About twenty browsing elephants were spread over a considerable stretch of land. The terrain was so difficult to survey that I couldn't make out more than the heads and backs of the adults, even with my field glasses. I had to maneuver still closer. One of the bulls drew himself up menacingly, spread his ears, and squinted at me, his eyes full of suspicion. With one of his forefeet, he fretfully scraped the ground. Having waited in vain for him to calm down, I finally tried to steal past him, sideways. To no avail. He came at me like a tank. Ten yards away, he veered off. The potent odor of elephant wafted in my direction. His impressive feint attack was meant to scare troublemakers away.

Since I didn't want to alarm the entire herd, I had little choice but to take his forceful hint and retreat. A while later, I tried my luck again and drove around the herd in another large curve. This time I came within fifty yards of the main group, and was immediately struck by the aggressive stance of one cow who stared at me, ready to charge. Half hidden in the grass between her legs, and dwarfed by her, was a dark figure. As I attempted to get my car into a better position, the excitable mother cow turned tail. The other animals followed. Not wanting to upset the herd further, I had to content myself with watching them through my binoculars. The cows eventually resumed their browsing. Through a few thin spots in the vegetation I succeeded in catching an occasional glimpse of the calf, who looked minuscule in comparison to his mother. At one point, he tried to suckle, stretching as high as he could to reach the source of milk hovering overhead. He bent his hind legs a little and lifted a front foot for better luck; but his success was short-lived, for the mother cow, still edgy, urged the herd onward.

The squadron of gray backs drifted slowly away, bobbing among the green waves of the bush. The herd was excited enough by the birth. So, as I didn't want to cause additional trouble, I remained behind. I hoped that during the next few days I would still be able to land a first by photographing the newborn calf. Elephants, after all, don't grow up overnight.

But I was disappointed. Three, four, five days passed. The terrain in the Endabash region is so complex that I was unable to locate the same group again, no matter how hard I tried. Nevertheless, some weeks later, I had a chance to photograph a calf that was barely a few days old, its hide still hanging like an ill-fitting coat about its shoulders, and sprouting long baby hair like a cactus. The calf seemed somewhat dazed and rarely ventured beyond its mother's legs. Standing under her belly when she took her daily shower, it, too, got soundly drenched. It had an older brother who drank all its milk. For whatever reason—an inflammation, perhaps—the mother cow denied one of her breasts to the two youngsters. This clearly benefited the older calf; the newborn had to wait its turn.

Elephant calves are born relatively large. Both baby males and females weigh about two hundred seventy pounds and measure an average of three feet at shoulder height. These giant infants need about ten quarts of milk each day. By the time they are one year old, they barely fit under their mother's belly. After losing their baby teeth when they are two or two and a half, they begin to grow tusks. This is about the right age for weaning, although it can vary greatly, depending on the tolerance of the individual cow. In most cases, complete weaning comes with the birth of the next calf; but certain cows allow their young to suckle even when they are six, seven, or eight years old, and they occasionally nurse two calves of disparate sizes simultaneously.

In contrast to most mammals, elephants' mammaries are located between their forelegs. I once observed a big calf, already endowed with sizable tusks, protesting vehemently when his mother attempted to educate him—his sharp tusks cruelly poked her between the ribs when he wanted to drink. But when she turned away, he made such a fuss, and so stubbornly followed the cow's every movement to get at her breast again, that she finally obliged. However, the time was nearing when his growing tusks would definitely prevent him from nursing.

Bulls display sexual behavior from tenderest childhood and mount each other as well as their female siblings with little regard for considerable differences in size. During their early years, calves are given tremendous leeway within their clan for tomfoolery. Adults and adolescents are willing to put up with a lot of nonsense. Toward evening, when the temperature begins to drop, the youngsters perk up. They elude maternal supervision and gather in little sandbox clubs. I once saw a small calf upset an entire herd with its bawling and carrying on as it ran around between the peacefully grazing animals. Alarmed by the possibility of danger, the cows rallied around the presumably threatened youngster, but the enemy was nowhere to be seen. The calf was merely proclaiming its exuberance.

When two family units meet, their respective calves grow particularly unruly. They run to meet each other, greet each other with outstretched trunks, sniff each other, skip around each other—and in no time at all, a lusty row is on.

One such afternoon encounter led to a violent fight between two three-year-olds. The pugnacious young bulls wrestled doggedly, twisting their trunks into impossible knots, bumping their heads, and trying desperately to push each other around. Each growled and groaned, slammed his forehead hard into his opponent's belly and behind, and was so absorbed in pulling the other's ears that he forgot the surrounding herds. Stopping to catch their breath, they suddenly found themselves alone. The two groups had long since parted and were going their opposite ways. The two hagglers saw them grazing at some distance and immediately gave up their belligerence, leaving their account unsettled, and ran with flapping ears and flying tails to catch up to their kin. One of the two heroes happened to come running in my direction. The sight of my Land-Rover seemed to increase his panic. He hollered and charged as if determined to trample the car into the ground, but changed his mind and instead vented his rage and anxiety on a shrub, knocking off some branches with his rear end, and then stormed at me again, screaming. The other elephants, alarmed, raised their heads and glowered at me. Though I knew myself to be perfectly innocent, I was embarrassed by the fuss. I felt as if I were trying to steal a baby's bottle and suddenly was caught by the child's governess. A youthful cow, probably the sister of the youngster who was charging at me, rushed to her little brother's aid, calmed him down, and led him safely back to the herd.

A lot of body contact shapes the mother-and-child relationship of elephants. The trunk, of course, is an important tactile instrument. Calves use their trunks to feel their mothers' bodies, to sample the menu by reaching into their mothers' mouths, and to savor their mothers' smell through these long olfactory tubes. Mother elephants, in turn, use theirs to guide their young and to soothe them when they are excited, either by putting their trunks into the youngsters' mouths or by fondling them—reassuring them of their maternal presence and imparting a feeling of security. Despite or perhaps because of their great physical strength, mother elephants are particularly gentle and kind to their calves. But they are by no means completely unselfish. During long periods of drought, when the rivers waste away and the watering places become dust pans, elephants resort to digging ground wells in the sandy riverbeds. Water collects very slowly in these sand holes. The impatient calves often can't wait, and push their trunks down to the bottom of the wells to drink their mothers' water, often causing the holes to collapse. The mother tries to keep her calf at bay until her thirst is quenched, pushing him or her aside with trunk and tusks, even blocking access to the hole with her body. If the thirsty calf is determined to get his way, the competition can go on for a long time. The calf often succeeds briefly, as the mother throws her head back to empty a trunkload of water into her gullet; but then he is instantly foiled again. On the whole, however, even these tests of patience remain on a friendly footing. Only once did I see a cow shoveling her calf aside with such an angry scoop of tusks that the youngster screamed in pain. Later I saw that he was bleeding from the mouth. Such violent cases are rare. In general, mothers and older sisters look after the small fry with loving care, as the following incident illustrates: A calf who had been wallowing in a mud hole to his heart's content couldn't scurry to solid ground. He kept floundering on his slippery feet and sliding back. Finally he squeaked for help. Mother and sister hurried to the rescue, hooked their trunks under his butt, and hoisted him out.

The strong bond between elephant mothers and their offspring was tellingly demonstrated in 1970 and 1971 when a bad drought in the Tsavo region took the lives of almost six thousand elephants, mainly cows and calves. The weakened calves severely curtailed the families' freedom of movement, keeping them close to the few remaining watering holes, in already depleted surroundings. Soon, even the cows were wasting away and, unwilling to abandon their dying young, eventually perished with them. The bulls, by contrast, had escaped in time to greener pastures and survived.

FURY DISPLACED

Driving along an elephant pass isn't easy. The pachyderms meticulously set one foot in front of the other on their treks, leaving a path hardly wider than fifteen or twenty inches—half as wide as a Land-Rover. The dense vegetation of the Endabash region makes following the narrow, curving path especially tricky. The best I could do was to plow through the bush.

I was trailing a group that I had discovered that morning around one of the watering holes and that now, in the early afternoon, was returning to the bush. I kept losing sight of them in the tall shrubbery. Time and again, I had to drive around impenetrable islands of thickets in the hope of finding the group on the other side. I had just forded a riverbed and was slowly forcing my way through a jungle of underbrush that girdled a clump of trees when, suddenly, I had an elephant before me.

He shrilled his trumpet and stormed my car, stomping down a few bushes in his path. But within six or seven yards, he stopped and turned instead to attack a young sapling that happened to be in his way. On this innocent little tree he vented the rage meant for my four-wheeled jalopy; his courage had failed him. Now, like a wrestler, he wound his trunk around the thin but resilient tree trunk and dragged it to the ground, trampling it. Then he remembered me, released the tree from his stranglehold, and stared at me. The pliable sapling bounced back into its original position. But the bull renewed his attack on the tree, rubbed his tusk against the wood, wheeled around, trampled the branches with his hind legs, trumpeted, scraped the bark with his ivories, and brought his opponent down a second time. He looked at me intensely from time to time, and the sight of me seemed to revive his fury. Again, he vented his awesome strength on the substitute foe, whose foliage was beginning to hang in tatters. Half crazed, he circled the tree, flinging his head about, his slapping ears sounding like the cracking of whips. He trumpeted, sent splintering wood flying, and trumpeted yet more wildly. A first-class temper tantrum. I was sweating. With a bit more courage, the bull might have demolished my Land-Rover. By now, the tree was uprooted. The bull picked up his defeated enemy, shook it, then tossed it aside. He attacked a few more shrubs in passing, crashed through the bushes, and disappeared. Seconds later, I saw his tusks gleaming between the branches to my left. Once more, he gestured threateningly, but avoided the decisive confrontation and was gone. This time, he didn't return. Only his ranting and raving reverberated throughout the landscape. Again and again I heard trumpet blasts from various directions, then silence.

On another occasion I saw an elephant vent her anger on a perfectly innocent surrogate rather than attack a dreaded enemy. This incident, too, took place in the prolific wilderness of the Endabash region. I was cautiously approaching a gathering of cows accompanied by only a few very young calves—part of a larger herd dispersed throughout a vast area. One cow objected to my spying. She shook her head, coiled her trunk up against her chest, and charged at me. Fortunately, within a few yards of my car she lost her courage. After a few indignant trumpet blasts, she stepped aside. For a while, I heard her trampling through the nearby thicket. Suddenly she attacked again from another direction and veered off just before hitting me. She repeated the attacks several times. Her last thrust was abruptly diverted by a rootstock. In a violent rage she tore it out, flipped it over her head, and disappeared into the bush.

The other elephants had ignored her display of temper and placidly continued to browse. Only an occasional solitary trumpet indicated that the enraged cow was still spoiling for a fight. And then I heard a clashing of tusks from the direction of her last signal. Cautiously I groped toward the noise. Each time I lost the track and stopped to get my bearings, I again heard the clashing of ivories. At the edge of an arid wallow, I found the cow. She was crossing swords with a huge bull and was obviously having fun. This time, she ignored me, no matter how close I ventured. The two behemoths, tusks locked, were pushing each other back and forth. In the end, the bull shoved the cow aside and encircled her shoulders with his trunk in a typical mating gesture. Now absorbed in

41

passionate games, they vanished into the bushes. The unmistakable agitation of the bull indicated that the cow was in heat, which in turn could explain her earlier repeated attacks.

A thunderstorm prevented me from further following the two elephants. With sudden vehemence, a curtain of rain descended, making the search impossible.

A VISITOR ON THE HOOD

One afternoon, I was sitting in my car, hidden between some shrubs at the edge of a wallow. The sun beat down mercilessly and the temperature was nearly 90° F. I felt like a steak broiling. The elephants were enjoying a cool bath, and I begrudged them every drop of water they squirted on their backs. But all I could do was watch the splashing, spraying, and snorting of their pleasurable ritual through my camera.

I was deep in contemplation of the idyllic scene when suddenly there was a soft knock on the Land-Rover's windshield. I looked up and was face to face with a snake, gracefully swaying its head on the other side of the glass! While I eyed it in surprise, it hissed a couple of times, showing its black, forked tongue. Having recovered from my initial shock—after all, it wasn't every day that I received this type of visitor on the hood of my car—I bent slightly forward to take a closer look at the reptile. It measured perhaps one and a half yards long and the fine-scaled skin on its back was the color of a light-green reed; its underbelly was white. I had no idea whether it was a poisonous snake, but it only had to wriggle about ten inches to the right in order to glide through the wide-open rectangle where I had removed the window and frame on the driver's side of the car. Naturally, I wasn't exactly delighted by this thought; for although it was no doubt a particularly beautiful specimen, I had no desire to get too intimately acquainted with a snake.

What could I do? Getting out of the car or starting the engine was out of the question; either would drive away the elephants I wanted to watch. The snake's searching head was again knocking on the windshield when I had an idea: I knocked back, in the same rhythm and just as softly. The result was baffling. The snake was as shocked as I had been when it first announced itself. It executed a few deft S-curves, slithered down the hood, and disappeared via a crack into the engine. Chances were it wouldn't bother me again. I sighed with relief and concentrated once again on my elephants.

That evening, I reported the incident at the camp. Friend Rashid's dark-skinned face lit up. "That's for good luck," he said, beaming. "We have a saying that goes: 'If a snake visits your hut or tent, it's a good omen; but if a lion is there, you're in trouble.'" That made sense. I felt lucky that a snake had mounted my hood and not a lion.

LITTLE INCIDENTS

In the southern part of Manyara National Park, the Endabash River has gnawed a gorge into the precipitous wall of the East African Rift. But at the height of the dry season, the Endabash was nothing more than a modest brook tumbling down to the valley and looking quite forlorn as it wound its way around the boulders piled up at the bottom of the gorge. After frothing down the final stretch of rapids, the waters quickly lost momentum and seeped into the ground. In the evenings, the elephants often came from the surrounding brush to drink at this spot. Having trouble moving about because of a badly swollen front leg, a sick bull was camping out in the vicinity of the watering place, the only one he could reach because of his infirmity. He spent his days in the shadow of the shrubs that fringed the foot of the rapids.

I wanted to find an observation post among the granite boulders above the water hole. A park ranger toting a rifle accompanied me on my search. We carefully picked our way around the lair of the sick elephant, who was dozing, and breathing as noisily as a diver drawing air through a snorkel. At the foot of the boulders, I took off my sandals to get a better grip on the rocks. We had barely reached the first ledge when the sick bull broke out of the bushes, got on our trail, and limped to the boulder where I had left my shoes. From the safety of our rocky perch, we saw him sniff one of my sandals and, with his trunk, abruptly send it sailing through the air, immediately followed by the second sandal. The ranger was grinning. Though briefly vexed by the cavalier fashion with which the elephant had dispensed with my belongings, I couldn't help suspecting that in the course of several years my shoes might well have acquired a smell peculiar enough to provoke even those whose noses are less sensitive than the long olfactory tract of an elephant. A bit embarrassed, I resolved never again to leave my sandals where an elephant might sniff them.

Aside from this episode, our expedition was a success. We found an ideal observation post exactly above the watering place. Yet, as luck would have it, the elephants on that day delayed their appearance until it was too dark for me to use my telephoto lens.

While waiting for the animals, I examined the ranger's rifle and was surprised to read, engraved on the lock, that it was an old Mauser, manufactured in 1909. I was being protected by a carbine from the arsenal of the last German kaiser's former colony in East Africa, and although I would have preferred to have seen it in an antique shop, I hesitantly asked the ranger whether he knew how to make the imperial contraption shoot. "Oh yes," he answered with a radiant smile, "it shoots like a cannon!" He paused to let his revelation sink in, while I cautiously pushed the weapon aside. Then he added: "But you needn't worry; I have no ammunition."

Experience has taught me—often the hard way—that elephants are extremely sensitive to unfamiliar sounds. The point was driven home when I was involved in the following episode in the Selous region: An island rose from the lake like the rounded shell of an outsized tortoise. On it grew one solitary tree and a few green bushes, in the middle of which stood a single bull elephant. As we approached the island, we turned off the motor of our boat. Ndege, our boatman, silently paddled us close to the shore. Sand faintly crunched under the keel as we beached the boat.

The bull elephant didn't seem to notice our arrival; at any rate, he paid no attention to us. Hiding among the few shrubs that fanned out between our landing place and the place where the bull was standing, I carefully sneaked closer, my camera ready, covered by a ranger who crouched behind me, his rifle unlocked. As we were downwind of the gray giant, I could come within ten yards of him without being detected. Slowly I straightened up, appraising the elephant through a gap in the shrubs. The bull, whose gleaming tusks contrasted to his dark hulk, was gathering fallen fruit with slow and deliberate movements. A perfect picture. I pushed the button on my camera—and the faint click was enough to startle him. He turned his head in my direction, raised his sail-like ears in alarm, stuck up his trunk, and sampled the air. It was a pose I couldn't miss. Because some branches were still spoiling the picture, I crept another yard closer. The bull turned his head from side to side suspiciously and stared straight at my camera. I pushed the button a second time. The click was feeble, but distinctly different from the sounds of an African morning. This time, the elephant was upset; and this time, he was also able to determine the direction of the disturbance. He immediately took steps to chase us. Fast steps! He came storming at me like a tank—a terrifyingly beautiful picture, if only I had had the time to capture it. But my legs ran away with me; I bolted like a rabbit. Clearly the stakes were higher than in the famous fable of the contest between the tortoise and the hare.

Ndege was already hastily readying the boat, and the ranger was running behind me. We were lucky. The bull did not insist on kicking us into the lake—camera, rifle, and all. It was enough to have taught us some respect. He stopped short, about ten or twelve yards from the boat. Ndege hadn't had the time to start the motor, and we drifted rather helplessly several yards offshore. The elephant could easily have sunk our fragile craft. Instead he stood at the water's edge, in all his splendor, and stared at us. He was once more the undisputed lord of the island.

FROM THE PORCH

I often spent my evenings sitting on the porch of my little *banda* (hut, in Swahili), watching the stars. At times, I also used the roof of the Land-Rover as a private observatory. Not that I was making exciting discoveries—though occasional shooting stars etching their fiery trails into the dark sky were exciting—but it was fun letting my imagination wander aimlessly among the shimmering dots. Some evenings, I was interrupted by the roaring of lions. Once, on a moonlit night, I could even make out the silhouettes of four predatory felines as they were passing by the wildlife observation post on their nightly hunt. Now and then, I heard the twanging voices of birds above me or saw a string of flamingoes making their rounds.

During my stay in Manyara I occupied two small rooms provided by the park administration. They were located in the right wing of the small group of buildings that constituted the wildlife observation post. My neighbors, three game wardens, patrolled the park on foot all day.

The post was built on an elevation that offered a fine view of the parklands and the lake. About two hundred yards to the right, the Musasa River rushed over a few rapids. Between the river and the *bandas* ran an elephant path leading into the narrow mountain valley that opened up behind the huts, between two hills. Some evenings, on my way home, I had to drive through an elephant herd grazing in front of the observation station before continuing on its way to the lush vegetation in the valley. Later, sitting on my porch and sipping my first cup of tea, I could enjoy a rare spectacle: Less than fifty yards off, a row of twenty or twenty-five elephants of all sizes, sometimes even more, would stride past almost without making a sound, seemingly unaware of the human presence nearby.

One night, I was awakened by soft scratching on the wall of my hut. I went outside quietly and in the beam of my flashlight caught a porcupine searching for leftovers. The animal wasn't the least bit bothered by the light, but kept busily rummaging around, at times only a yard from my legs. When I stepped out of its way, accidentally kicking a trash bin, the clang frightened my nocturnal visitor so thoroughly that it ran off in panic. Long after it had disap-

47

peared, I could tell where it was running by the rhythmic rattling of its quills. Another time, I awoke at the sound of heavy breathing and of grass being plucked. From my doorway I saw two elephants raiding the front yard in the moonlight.

I shared my hut itself with certain tenants from the animal kingdom. Swallows nested under the eaves and went sailing with shrill twitter above my head while I was having breakfast, and a tribe of rock agamas dwelled under the rafters next to the geckoes, who flitted up and down the walls at night, hunting mosquitoes. Sometimes I heard these lizards rustle in my pantry, and occasionally there was a loud thumping on the tin roof when a crimson-headed male of the species was wildly chasing a female.

Twice a week, I made a shopping and refueling trip to Mto-Wa-Mbu, a small settlement at the northern tip of Lake Manyara, a few miles from the park entrance. No matter how stubbornly I bargained for my bananas, tomatoes, and onions, the greengrocers always ended up the winners. Water and gasoline had to be lugged home in barrels. On one occasion, a zealous gas station attendant mixed these two basic necessities right in my tank. That day, I had trouble getting home at all. I had to dismantle and clean the carburetor and filter several times before I finally reached the ranger station, the engine still sputtering.

AT THE WATERING PLACE

A phalanx of gray elephants—twelve in all—was standing along the banks of the Musasa River. At irregular intervals the animals lowered their trunks to suck up water, raised their heads, and, putting their trunks in their

48

mouths, let the water run slowly into their gullets. A mature elephant can drink as much as ten quarts of water with each trunkful; his daily requirement, however, exceeds one hundred quarts.

Each animal was pouring ten or more trunkfuls down its throat to quench its thirst. Between drinks, a few of the behemoths were squirting each other for the fun of it. Some pressed their two opposing trunk fingers together so that jets of water sprang sideways from the now double opening. Others used their trunks to strafe the river's surface and whip up broad fans of water.

Two calves, less than a year old, simply dangled their hoses in the reddish waves. Obviously trying to imitate their elders, but without understanding the complex mechanism of drinking, they were helpless and impatient. One of them finally hit upon the idea of putting his dripping trunk into his mouth and sucking it—a first step in the learning process that, after much practice, would lead to mastery. The other calf, driven by thirst, lowered his head all the way down to the water to drink directly with his mouth, one hind leg sticking up into the air to counterbalance this difficult, top-heavy position.

Baby elephants are not born with the ability to make full use of their versatile trunk. It takes constant training for them to master the countless possibilities of their nose muscles. The trunk acts as arm, hand, water pump, mudsling, wind gauge, radar, lumber crane, and more, much more. . . . It is a supreme masterpiece of evolution, which, by combining nose and upper lip, developed an organ whose agility is only equaled by—and sometimes is superior to—that of the human arm. The vast range of its possible uses, from the precise plucking of a single blade of grass to the toppling of a full-grown tree, results from the interplay of several thousand muscles. The coordination of these muscles takes diligent training. Very young calves can therefore often be seen helplessly flinging their trunks about, and sometimes even trampling on them.

At the watering place I was amazed by one of the bulls, for he had learned an unusual drinking trick. Like all the others, he first filled up his trunk, then squirted the water down his gullet; but unlike the others, he finished it off with a few flips of his looped trunk, as if to shake his nose empty of the last drop. He repeated the distinctive flourishes after every drink.

The group moved slowly away. Only one bull, perhaps twenty to twenty-five years old, lingered. He knelt down in the water, rolled to the side, completely submerged himself, came up again, and, swinging his trunk, got up; then he pried loose a few chunks of earth, threw some of them over his back, and swallowed the others. Standing at the very edge of a small flat ledge that projected into the river, he abruptly began to step so forcefully into the waves with his left forefoot that massive sheets of water spattered against his belly. To keep the waves agitated, he repeated the procedure at regular intervals, constantly shifting position to use a different leg each time. With his hind legs, in particular, he sent curtains of water splashing around him. In between, he stirred the mud with wide, circular swings of his trunk. Then he slid into the water again to wallow in another full bath. Back near the shore, he whipped up a fresh little storm around his legs. In all, he enjoyed more than an hour of solitary fun.

The other peacefully browsing elephants had already crossed through the woods that bordered the river and had wandered out onto the beach—a treeless strip of sand—that girdled the lake. Meanwhile, two other groups of elephants were slowly approaching. When the three groups met, there was a welcoming ceremony of sniffing and trunk-touching. Finally the three families mingled into one herd of perhaps forty or fifty animals of various ages.

Nearby, a wallow marked the spot where the Musasa River flowed into the lake. Two adolescent bulls reached this water hole first and promptly began to collect ammunition with their trunks for a mudslinging contest, soundly peppering each other with the dirt. As if that weren't enough, the smaller of the two suddenly plopped on his knees and, using his feet and tusks, burrowed deeper and deeper into the mire. The other joined in immediately. As if churning in a huge tub of butter, the two bulls, kicking and rolling, made every blubbering, spattering, burping, smacking, or squishing noise to attract their companions. A few cows led their calves to the wallow. The youngsters flung themselves on their bellies and skidded spread-eagle through the slippery mess, rolled over, smeared their heads with the gooey paste, and slithered their trunks like eels through the muck.

More and more elephants kept arriving to coat themselves liberally with mud, as if to spruce up their gray old facades with fresh plaster. The wallow was soon overflowing with bodies—ears, trunks, legs, and tusks in wild profusion. A large bull came stalking up and elbowed in as if taking his right-of-way for granted, shoving the two adolescents aside and plopping down, the black slime oozing up around his groin. He, too, rolled over and plastered himself so thoroughly with mud that finally only the whites of his eyes were glinting through a mask of clay. After a while, he laboriously propped himself up like a dog on his front legs, paused, drew his hind legs under him, and heaved himself into an upright position. At last he was standing safely on all fours, his legs looking like pillars of concrete arising from the bog.

The place he vacated was at once taken by a cow and her

half-grown young, who joined the general press at the wallow. They left ten minutes later, freshly plastered. After a few steps, the cow stumbled across a short, thick stick, picked it up like a brush by its handle with her trunk fingers, and used it to scratch her chest. Then she carelessly dropped it to concentrate on some tufts of grass. I have often watched elephants use such tools. On one occasion I saw a bull scratching his flanks with a palm frond. On another, a young cow selected a branch to scrape herself. Time and again, an elephant will accidentally discover that a stick can be an extension of his trunk and will remember the lesson when he happens to see a stick that seems to fit the bill. The use of tools for personal hygiene, although not widespread among elephants, certainly demonstrates the versatility of an elephant's trunk.

An old bull showed me the following interesting variations on personal hygiene: Having thoroughly scrubbed every inch of his body against the rough surface of a termite hill, he dozed off for a few minutes, then gave a sudden start, probably inconvenienced by a tickle in his nose. He slipped his left nostril about six or seven inches over one of his tusks, picking his nose by twisting his trunk back and forth. Then he repeated the procedure, screwing his tusk up the right nostril. I was to observe this method of nose-cleaning many more times and concluded that dust, sand, and plant particles must frequently get trapped in an elephant's trunk and irritate it.

Elephants are also severely plagued by ticks, especially in the folds around the mouth, under and on the trunk, and behind the ears. The parasites bore their heads into the pachyderms' skin, which, although it has the appearance of wrinkled leather, is by no means as thick as it looks. Having filled themselves with blood, the "ripe" ticks hang from the host animal like yellow-brown berries. Eventually, they drop by themselves or are crushed when the elephants rub themselves against trees or termite hills after their mud baths. I once watched an elephant trying to remove a tick that had drilled itself into his chin. He delicately grasped it with his trunk fingers and pulled it with care; but he failed in his repeated attempts and lost the tug-of-war to the insect. The bite of a horsefly or one of the myriad tsetse flies can anger a young calf. Clearly, the daily mud bath serves above all to provide a protective coating against these vermin and their painful attacks.

Having finished their mud baths, the elephants crossed over to a dead tree. I could tell by its smoothly polished trunk that elephants frequently came this way and never missed the occasion to use the tree for a good scrub. One mud-plastered bull, black as night itself in his slippery splendor, first used the scrubbing post behind his ears; after several rubs, he scratched his right shoulder, then his left; finally he concentrated so vigorously on his rear end that the tree began to sway. A few paces away was another tree, toppled. Its main branch was sticking out sideways at about half the height of an elephant, making it an ideal scrubbing stand. The bull strolled over, laid his head on the branch, and scratched himself under the chin. Then he took the wood between his forelegs to sand down his skin above the breastbone. Gradually, all the elephants came by for an equally thorough massage. The beauty routine ended when the animals powdered their backs, sides, and underbellies with dust, applying the finishing touch to the thick mud crust that would protect them from insects and heat. Using their forefeet, they piled up a little heap of dust, ladled it up with their trunks, and fired it like cannonballs, the dust billowing around them.

Little by little, the dust drifted away. The elephants resumed their browsing, pulling bunches of grass from the ground and carefully beating them two or three times against their chests to shake off much of the earth before chewing up the grass.

The sun was sinking. A little breeze blew in from the lake; the day began to cool. The young perked up. Like a gang of feisty teenagers, they began cruising around. One little bull broke away from his peers, flapped his ears, spun like a top, and suddenly blew his trumpet so shrilly it seemed as if he meant to rout a pack of lions. But no one paid much attention. So he ran back to his pals, grabbed one of them around the back, and tried to wrestle him down. The attacked elephant deftly extricated himself, wheeled around, and slung his trunk around his opponent's, trying with all his might to force him back. Their trunks were pressed upright, the undersides touching. The little fellows were fighting their first duels using exactly the same posture with which adults settle disputes of rank.

Another calf now discovered a handy branch to play with. He wrapped his trunk around the stick, stood it on its end, kicked it, dropped it, and, grabbing it at a different spot, picked it up once more. His quiet play was soon being watched. One of his companions came up, snatched the other end of the stick, and after a brief tug-of-war the toy changed hands. The winner, however, had little use for it, dragged it a few steps, and dropped it.

Several cattle egrets were walking among the elephants, catching the insects disturbed by the herd's arrival. Suddenly a small bull, his ears spread, lit into the white birds with such determination that he drove them off—only to see them alight again not far off. Another calf found a vulture's feather. He put the quill into his mouth and flaunted it for a while. Then he took it between his trunk fingers and swung it like a little flag. But as soon as he spotted two young bulls haggling, he negligently dropped his prize and proceeded in all innocence to mount one of the wrestlers. The victim went down on his knees under the surprise assault and rolled over, which caused him to lose the skirmish up front. His playmates immediately stepped on his flanks in the classical pose of the victor. At last, the beleaguered loser was allowed to struggle to his feet.

TUMBLING INTO THE WORLD

The elephants were strolling leisurely through the acacia forest, haphazardly plucking a few leaves, tearing out bunches of grass, breaking the branches of treetops. I followed the herd through the afternoon. Suddenly the long neck of a giraffe appeared above the bushes. She attentively watched the approach of the pachyderms; then she turned and withdrew deeper into the thicket. That was when I saw the two white dots on her behind. Could it be that ...? It was indeed. The white-hoofed tips of a calf's front feet were sticking out of her body!

I became very excited. How many people have been lucky enough to watch—let alone to photograph—the birth of a giraffe in the wild? Photographing the elephants was put aside for the rest of the day. I checked the sun: approximately 4:30 P.M. Two more hours of daylight! I drove carefully around in the brush, looking for an appropriate place to stop.

A gap in the foliage soon gave me a good view of the birthing giraffe. She was standing in a small clearing surrounded by shrubs. A series of contractions rippled through her body; she bent her neck forward and opened her mouth a little. As soon as the contractions subsided, she raised her head again and looked around. An elephant bull suddenly broke through the brush and eyed the cow with curiosity. She moved a few steps to get out of his way, but then stood still. The elephant swung his trunk several times in her direction, but a few minutes later he continued on his way as though he didn't want to disturb her.

Unfortunately, she was now half hidden from my view. Very slowly, letting the clutch slip, I rolled the car to a better observation spot. The giraffe looked at me warily, but didn't budge. Ten minutes later, her labor pains began again. Then the oblong head of the calf appeared. To my surprise, it seemed almost black. The characteristic horn cones were barely visible, folded flat against the skull. Once in a while, the head moved. Another pause. The giraffe lowered her head and chewed a few leaves from the shrubs. The next wave of pains had barely begun when she threw her head up and stared fearfully past me.

I heard the breaking of branches. Sounds of heavy trampling and a puffing like that of an old steam engine were getting louder. Within seconds a rhinoceros broke through the underbrush, followed by a very young calf. Horns drooping, the rhino trotted along the path that led directly to the giraffe, whose newborn was already dangling half out of her womb. I swore under my breath. I hadn't sighted a rhino for weeks, and now, of all things, this leviathan came blustering into the picture.

The giraffe was taking a few nervous steps when the rhino stopped: She had seen my car! Her small eyes blinked, searching. Our shock was mutual, but brief. Then the rhino spun around and stormed off, the calf at her heels. I sighed with relief. What a double hit it would have been to be rammed by a rhino during the birth of a giraffe!

But however glad I was about my narrow escape, I now had a problem: The rhino's surprise visit had upset the giraffe; she turned around, and I could no longer photograph the birthing. I hardly had time to change position again, and besides, I didn't want to be a nuisance to the mother during the final phase of her delivery.

Pushed by the contractions and pulled by its own weight, the calf's hindquarters glided faster and faster out of the birth canal. At last, the newcomer tumbled—in the fullest sense of the word—into the world, hitting the ground with a thud and then lying there as if it were dead. The birth, as far as I had been able to watch, beginning with the protrusion of the front hooves, had taken roughly forty minutes.

The tumble had snapped the umbilical cord. At once, the birth sac, dangling between the giraffe's hind legs, began to fill with a bright red fluid from her womb. It soon looked like an enormous red balloon. Two or three minutes later, the cow turned to her calf. She spread her forelegs, lowered her head, and smelled the newborn, then gently peeled away the white embryonic membrane that still covered parts of its body. She lifted her head again to read the wind. Moments later, the calf showed the first signs of life: It tried to raise its head, but quickly had to let it sink to the ground. A little later, the head again came up from the grass, swaying, like a cobra, on the wobbly neck. Once more, the giraffe bent down, licked her calf across the forehead, and straightened up. Little by little, she cleansed the baby's shoulders and rump, giving the anal region extra attention. This treatment clearly stimulated the calf, and although it still had trouble keeping its head and neck up, it now attempted to get on its forelegs. Just as it was about to prop itself up on widespread limbs, it lost its balance and plopped back into the grass.

As I was busy putting a fresh roll of film in my camera, I heard a thud and a splash: The red balloon had dropped to the ground and burst. A short time later, the calf's second attempt at getting up ended miserably in the grass. So did the third and fourth. In between, the mother renewed her encouragement, licking and prodding her offspring with her tongue. And at long last, after a few more failures had taught the calf to lean its neck against the long limbs of its mother, it got up on its forelegs, struggled slowly to its hind legs—and was standing! Head precariously balanced, knees buckling, it cut a pitiful figure; but at least it stood on its own legs. Within seconds, it attempted its first step, promptly lost balance, and landed once more in the grass. But a moment later, it was standing again.

About one hour had elapsed from the moment of the calf's tumbling into the world to its first attempt at standing up. Now it was uncertainly stalking about between its mother's legs, trying to find its bearings. The cow continued to lick it now and then and, with her head and forelegs, tried as best she could to guide it to her teats. The youngster sniffed at all imaginable parts of the large maternal body, its soft mouth bumping searchingly against her chest; it tugged at her tail and examined some remains of the afterbirth still hanging about her hindquarters. But, hungry as it evidently was, it simply couldn't find the mammaries. The giraffe stepped up to the nearest bush and started to eat. The calf followed clumsily and resumed its fumbling. At one point, its lips actually touched her teats, but it wouldn't drink. It continued its search until nightfall without discovering the fountain of life.

Three days went by before I met the mother and child again. The calf was doing fine. Its filly-like movements were still angular, but it could now keep up with its mother. When I came too close, it scampered nimbly away.

BIRDS, BEETLES, BEHEMOTHS

During countless rainy seasons the river had gnawed deeper and deeper into the earth. Torrents had created cliffs, and kingfishers had carved their nest holes into the bluff. These colorful insect hunters often perched on the stump of a dead tree that arched out over the water. Now and then, one of the birds, looking like an arrowhead with some red feathers glued to it, shot down to the river. It dipped quickly into the waves, bounced up, and darted back to its post—usually with an empty beak. But sometimes a small fish, a dragonfly, or a grasshopper would be wriggling in its wedge-shaped bill.

I once watched one of these iridescent dive bombers carve up a grasshopper I had thought far too big for the tiny bird. It kept beating its prey against a branch until all the unwieldy parts such as the legs and the wings had fallen off. Then it let the insect, a huge hunk, glide into its gullet, headfirst. The grasshopper went down slowly. Finally the bird clapped its bill open and shut a few times. Finished. Another time I saw a kingfisher hunt above unusually rich fishing grounds. Within five minutes of repeated diving, it returned three times with a fish in its bill. After gobbling the third fish, it took time off to carefully rearrange its feathers.

One night, a group of elephants descended to the river valley. Placidly browsing, the animals approached the nesting place of the kingfishers. Two adolescent calves suddenly started a fight. They were shoving and pushing each other closer and closer to the nest openings in the bluff. The stronger bull finally pinned his opponent against the wall. The birds, obviously worried for their brood, flitted and twittered excitedly above the two warriors, who paid them absolutely no heed. In gallant defense of its nest hole, one of the

59

kingfishers even alighted on the back of one of the pachyderms, but to no avail. Fortunately, the elephants did little damage except for rubbing some sand off the wall of the cliff with their coarse skin. As soon as the fight moved into open terrain, the birds darted to their caves and disappeared through the dark openings. A little while later, they reappeared one after the other, chirping and screeching, and now flew to their accustomed haunts in the surrounding shrub, where they preened their feathers. The hatchery clearly had survived the upheaval.

A few hundred yards downstream I found another family—elephants grazing along the precipitous riverbank. The lead cow spent considerable time trying to uproot a bush that was partially hanging over the embankment. Then she descended the almost vertical embankment wall, which was at least six feet high. She accomplished this unusual mountaineering feat by lying on her belly and, with her forefeet stretched in front of her, sliding down the steep slope till she felt the ground below her and could lower the rest of her body and her hind legs. Two other members of her clan, convinced that there was no better way, also tobogganed down the incline on their bellies. The rest of the group took a short detour.

My Land-Rover was settled like a boulder between the bushes. The elephants approached it without fear and stepped nonchalantly around it. Two cows came particularly close, each leading a calf hardly more than a year old. One of them, a young bull, recognized the car as an object foreign to his environment and wanted to satisfy his curiosity. He stopped briefly, within eight yards of the vehicle, raised his trunk, sniffed the air, took a few steps toward me, stopped again, skeptically swayed his head, swung his trunk back and forth hoping to pick up an explanatory scent, and rolled his eyes, drawing still nearer.

Then he plucked up his courage and edged close enough to touch the car with his outstretched trunk. He was still puzzled. But the strange object didn't fill him with undue anxiety, for after a few seconds he walked away with the air of an adventurer returning home after a successful expedition, his self-esteem intact.

One of the bulls spread his hind legs, raised his tail, and dropped eight soft balls, one after the other, accompanied by a gushing waterfall. Fifteen to twenty pounds of solid body waste and perhaps ten quarts of fluid were being dumped. Throughout the afternoon, the elephants deposited piles of dung on various spots that reminded me of those pyramids of ammunition stacked next to medieval cannons.

The elephant manure attracted hordes of scarab beetles, who burrowed into it and kneaded their own little balls from the stuff. In the vicinity of a termite hill, a beetle was struggling to push up a slope one of his creations that was as big as a tennis ball. He was walking in reverse, using his hind legs to coax the ball uphill. But the going was tough; the ball frequently escaped sideways and rolled back down the slope a little. Nonetheless, the beetle seemed to know exactly where he was heading, and the repeated mishaps didn't faze him. Undaunted, he retrieved the ball each time and rolled it uphill again, following exactly the same route. His Sisyphean labor was crowned with success when he and his round freight finally disappeared into a tangle of roots. A few days later, I saw the same procedure in reverse, when two beetles struggled to transport their newly kneaded dung ball downhill. The female clung to the ball in typical female-beetle fashion, while the male did the rolling and steering. But soon the ball started to roll faster than the male beetle could push it. Then the male, too, got aboard, and the dung ball, with two stowaways holding on for dear life, rolled faster and faster to the foot of the slope fifteen feet below, where the male resumed pushing it through the grass before burying it at the planned spot.

An adult elephant drops about two hundred pounds of excrement every twenty-four hours. A group of ten adults therefore distributes more than a ton of first-rate organic fertilizer across the land each day. From the biochemist's point of view, a large elephant herd is like an ambulatory fertilizer factory and plays an essential part in the metabolism—energy budget within an ecological system. Elephants are known to digest their food poorly. Only twenty percent of what they eat is actually converted into energy; the remaining eighty percent is valuable organic waste to be recycled.

The recycling of these waste materials is largely done by the scarab beetles, whose whole existence depends on dung balls. There are more than two thousand kinds of such dung beetles in Africa alone, and some of them specialize in elephant dung. The pachyderms' droppings yield food aplenty for countless hordes of scarabs. Some of them flatten the dung into large cakes; others knead it into smaller balls that they bury in the ground within ten to twenty yards of the source. This activity, repeated millions of times each day, processes tons of manure, breaking it up into small doses and distributing it more or less evenly over large areas, efficiently fertilizing the soil of an area. The dung provides the scarabs not only with food, but with nurseries as well. The female deposits her eggs into the dung before the male buries it. The young brood must eat their way through a spherical dung patch before they can see the light of day.

The dung beetle, in turn, is of interest to the iguanas in this ecological cycle. One afternoon, I observed an iguana creeping out from under some bushes and heading straight for a pile of dung balls. The lizard measured perhaps a yard from his head to the tip of his tail. Upon reaching his goal, he immediately set about tearing the elephants' souvenir apart with his sharp claws. I was baffled at first, until I discovered that the iguana didn't care so much for the dung as for the beetles housed inside it.

I was to meet another of these lizards during my stay. He, too, was burrowing in a dung heap and was so intent upon catching beetles that he didn't hear my approach. My car was already within a few yards of him when he quickly bolted, scurried off as fast as a weasel, and flitted past an elephant who in turn got upset and threatened pursuit. The lizard scurried still faster, splashed noisily into a pool, wriggled across to the opposite shore, climbed the embankment, and disappeared into the safety of the dense scrub.

TWINS?

One afternoon, as I caught up with a family of elephants I had seen only a few times before, I was struck by the sight of two calves of exactly the same size who were traveling together. As the tips of their tusks were not yet visible, I guessed that they were about two and a half years old. I simply couldn't tell the two little bulls apart. I became more interested in them as one of the pair ran to his mother and started to drink. The second followed promptly and wanted to drink from the cow's other udder. At first the cow shooed him off; then she relented. For several minutes the two young bulls stood almost symmetrically right and left of the cow and filled their bellies. Later, as they were standing side by side plucking leaves from a bush, I took another careful look at them. But no matter how methodically I compared them, I could find no difference in size. Could I have found twins?

Twins are a rare phenomenon among elephants. Although

the British zoologist Richard Laws has concluded from his examination of the uteruses of dead elephant cows that the probability rate for twin births is as high as 1:100, only two such cases have been recorded to date. In 1976, Iain and Oria Douglas-Hamilton found a set of elephant twins in Manyara National Park. Unfortunately, one of the two calves did not survive the extreme drought of that year. The other pair were born in 1980 in Amboselia Park in Kenya and have been watched by the American elephant researcher Cynthia Moss from the moment of their birth.

The family of "my" twins included three adult cows. One of them had a calf who was approximately six months old. The second was the lead cow, whom I took to be the twins' mother. But the matter was complicated by the fact that the third cow, too, clearly had milk in her mammaries. Yet there were only two other calves, both adolescents, perhaps seven or eight years old.

The next morning I searched for some time before finding the group two to three miles from the place where I had left them. Again, I saw the two calves drink from the lead cow; this time, the cow didn't object. During the next hour I saw a replay of what I had seen the day before. The two calves stayed close together and generally remained near the lead cow.

That afternoon, my joy at the discovery of twins burst like a soap bubble. I saw one of the calves drink from the third cow. However, the false twin soon joined his "brother," and both youngsters spent the rest of the day together, near the lead cow. A half hour before dark, I was again elated. The calves once more were standing right and left of the lead cow and drinking at her teats. The following morning I discovered the group beneath an acacia tree from which they had torn several branches. The lead cow finished her branch off in a matter of minutes, then eyed the tree again. The other cows, noticing that she was insatiable, turned their backs to her and tried to drag their branches beyond the reach of her trunk. Sure enough, the lead cow made an attempt at appropriating another cow's greens, but she met with such determined opposition that she decided to reach into the treetop instead. First she tugged at some shoots, then wound the tip of her trunk around a branch for a better grip and pulled the branch down.

The elephants had been feeding from the tree for nearly an hour when a second group appeared and showed interest in the same feeding place. At first, both groups tried silently to stare each other down; then the two lead cows made menacing gestures to impress each other. But the tension subsided, and in the end both families closed in on the already somewhat tattered acacia. The family with the twins, however, soon found the place too crowded and strolled off to a cluster of shrubs. There the cows immediately resumed feeding while the calves played.

The youngest calf repeatedly rammed his head into the rear end of one of the twins, as if meaning to push him aside. The twin tried to fend off the impertinent cub with a sharp kick; but when his playmate persisted, he spun around and in turn butted his head into the behind of the fleeing little calf. Suddenly, the mother of the little calf turned around and told the twin off with an impatient punch of her tusks. The startled twin screamed and hastily withdrew to a safe distance.

That day I saw the twins drink from the lead cow on two occasions. Both times the cow showed no partiality. During the next few days the scene was repeated several times. On one occasion, one of the twins happened to be standing next to the other lactating cow. When his companion started to drink from the lead cow, he nevertheless immediately ran to join him and started to suckle, too. The drinking habits of the pair suggested that I had indeed discovered a set of twins—an assumption buttressed by the fact that even when the two calves strayed far from the lead cow, they were almost always inseparable. Still, I was never completely certain, particularly because on three occasions I caught one of the twins suckling from the "wrong" cow—and I had no way of knowing whether it was the same twin each time.

Back in Nairobi when Cynthia Moss and I swapped experiences concerning "her" twins and "mine," she shared my conviction and understood my doubts. I regret that I couldn't have observed the interesting pair for a longer period, but I could hardly abandon all other photographic projects in Manyara just because I had unexpectedly discovered twins. Besides, the pair appeared so strong and healthy that I could always hope to meet them again at some later date.

RAIN AT LAST!

Thunderclouds had been piling up in the evening sky for days. Time and again, sheet lightning flared through the dusk and hot, still air brooded over the savannah. The arid earth had burst in many places, a network of cracks crisscrossing the ground. Dust whirled up at the slightest breath of air. The last water holes had long since dried up; the mud wallows were baked and crusted, forming strange reliefs. The elephants had to dig their holes deeper and deeper into the sand of dried-up riverbeds for a trickle of water. It took a long time before the holes collected enough to fill an elephant's trunk. The sun had singed the grass; half-withered twigs hung from the trees.

One afternoon, a black wall of clouds rolled in from the east. Lightning flashed, and thunder growled across the plain. The first gusts of wind swept the land, driving dust columns and tangled balls of dead shrubbery before them. The wind carried the smell of rain—the earthy, liberating smell that wells up when a first shower drenches the thirsty soil. A few raindrops fell, bursting in the dust like overripe cherries splattering on the ground. Little dust puffs sprang up where the drops hit the dry earth. The rain intensified. Tiny fountains pulsated everywhere from the ground. Soon the thundershower poured down like a waterfall, flooding the thirsty land.

The elephants, who had roamed far and wide in search of food among the bushes, now stood tightly packed together as the ground was quickly covered by several inches of water. The animals patiently weathered the cloudburst that came rattling down on them; meanwhile, they filled their trunks with fresh rainwater. Some small calves ran excitedly about. They fanned the air with their ears, swung their trunks, spun around in circles, splashed through puddles, dipped their trunks into the flood, and puffed and snorted exuberantly.

One pit of the wallow had already become a pool. Four calves, one by one, slipped over its frothy edge and down into the fresh bath. They rolled, tussled, and wriggled in the mud, stuck their legs into the air, squeaked and trumpeted into the rain, attempted to climb out, skidded, and slid back into the pit. A few adult animals joined in the fun and plunged into the warm rainwater. Two adolescent bulls were wrestling playfully at the edge of the wallow. One of them stepped back, slipped and landed on his butt, paddled helplessly around in the slime, and at last regained his footing. The tremendous excitement that had seized the herd when the storm began gradually subsided.

The elephants had quenched their thirst and had enjoyed a heavenly shower. Now they dispersed again to continue browsing in the brush.

I did what I could to dry the several cameras I had used to record these jolly rites of spring. Unfortunately I hadn't expected it to rain on that day and had, as usual, set out without taking along the two side windows that I had removed from the Land-Rover to make picture-taking easier. Of course I had been unable to resist photographing the pachyderms during the downpour instead of taking shelter in the rear of the car and waiting for the storm to blow over. As a result, I was soaked to the bone, was shivering like a wet cat, and felt punished for my negligence. But I figured it was a small price to pay for participating in the elephants' rain festival.

UNEASY NEIGHBORS

Except for people, who have become their most unnatural enemy, elephants have no natural enemies. Mature elephants, that is. Young calves can sometimes fall victim to lions or hyenas. Ordinarily, elephant families keep their calves from ending up between the jaws of a lion pack, but any sick or orphaned calf that stays behind his herd will soon attract the rapacious felines' attention. Several reports of lions attacking young elephants are on record. One comes from the Luangwa Valley in Zambia, where a lion pulled a calf to the ground and killed him with one bite on the throat. The victim's tusks were already nearly a foot long. In Uganda, on the other hand, zoologist C. A. Timmer observed a lioness trying to kill an elephant calf. She ended up impaled on a tusk.

The number of elephant deaths due to predators is so negligible that it is not even listed among statistical causes of death—which doesn't mean that elephants never become the sumptuous repast of lions. Far from being only a hunter, the king of beasts is occasionally a shameless looter of corpses. Early one morning, in a little clearing cut into a palm thicket, I found a lioness busy ripping intestines from the corpse of an elephant cow. The feline must have been feeding on the carcass before the crack of dawn, for her belly was already bulging. I had driven past that exact spot the afternoon before and had noticed nothing unusual. Therefore the cow must have died during the night, perhaps of a lung disease that at the time had killed several elephants in Manyara National Park.

I discovered the rest of the pack of lions lying among the bushes a few hundred yards from the dead cow, all of them equally well stuffed, lolling about in the morning sun without a care in the world. They wouldn't have to go hunting for several days to come. When the heat intensified, they retreated into the broad branches of an umbrella acacia, where they rested comfortably until evening. Then they were ready for a second elephant banquet.

The lions of Manyara National Park love climbing trees and whiling away whole afternoons in the branches. But the trees offer more than shelter from heat and mosquitoes. Occasionally, they also offer refuge from the elephants. Elephants don't care for lions and conversely lions prefer to stay clear of elephants. Many a lion cub has saved his life by fleeing up a tree when pursued by enraged pachyderms.

THERE'S MORE TO AN ELEPHANT THAN MEETS THE EYE

The bull was coming at me, ears spread menacingly. Abruptly, within yards of my Land-Rover, he stopped and headed for the bushes, head high. The sight of an elephant attacking full sail is so terrifying that most of his enemies will take to their heels at the giant's first steps.

Evolution has endowed the elephant with huge ears not so much to help him intimidate his adversaries, or to equip him with an instrument so sensitive he could almost hear grass grow, but to protect him from heat stroke under the hot African sun. For an elephant's ears represent a highly efficient cooling system. They are shot through with a bundle of large arteries branching off into increasingly smaller blood vessels. When the elephant moves his ears, the fanning motion generates an air current, cooling his blood, which is circulating close to the skin surface. With the help of a transmitter tied around the neck of an elephant that had been tranquilized, Iain Douglas-Hamilton established that the blood pumped into this cooling network through the large artery and the blood leaving the ear through the veins can differ several degrees Fahrenheit in temperature, depending on the elephant's activity. An elephant easily adjusts his cooling system to the changes in his environment throughout the day. He simply has to fan quickly or slowly with his ears. At night, or during the cool morning and evening hours, he doesn't have to fan as much as during the hot hours of the day, which he spends mostly in the shade of trees. In cases of extreme exertion, for instance in flight, he can cool himself further by burping up water from his stomach and using his trunk to hose it over his shoulders and ears.

An elephant's tusks, in addition to his ears, possess remarkable features. Constantly worn down by daily use, they grow throughout his entire life. In adult cows, each tusk may weigh forty-five pounds on the average. In bulls, they can easily weigh two or three times as much, or more. The heaviest elephant tusk on record weighed two hundred twenty-five pounds and measured twenty-six feet long. It came from a bull shot in 1899 in the Kilimanjaro region. The tusks of Ahmed, a legendary bull who lived in the Marsabit area of Kenya until his death in 1974, and whose life-sized memorial stands guard in front of Nairobi's National Museum, also weighed in at almost two hundred twenty pounds each. Unfortunately, this kind of "big tusker"—as it is called in the hunting jargon of East Africa—has become exceedingly rare as a result of the boom in the ivory trade.

Just as there are right- and left-handed humans, elephants prefer to use their right or left tusk for their daily chores—and their tusks wear off accordingly. In many cases it is possible to tell right-tuskers from left-tuskers by a notch mark immediately above the tip of the more frequently used tusk. These notches, which can be distinctive, result from the elephant's using his tusk as a lever when pulling bundles of grass from the earth. Day after day, grass is loosened with the same well-practiced prying motion and pulled across the same spot on the tusk, creating a groove in it that becomes quite deep over the years. Only two-thirds of the tusk, from the tip up, is solid ivory; the hollow third near the root houses the nerve.

Next to an elephant's trunk and the size of his body, his tusks are doubtless his most striking feature. But the teeth inside his mouth are just as interesting and important. In the final analysis, the teeth determine how long an elephant will live. Only one molar at a time can grow in each of the two upper and two lower sides of an elephant's jaws. Constant chewing of food not only wears the molar down, but gradually causes it to lean forward along the ridge of the jawbone while a new molar is growing in eventually to replace it altogether. Only six such sets of molars can grow in during the span of an elephant's life. Once the last set of four molars is worn down, the elephant can no longer chew properly. Even surrounded by the lushest vegetation, he slowly and surely starves to death, an event that normally takes place at the time when he has

71

reached an age of fifty-five or sixty.

An elephant herd constantly emits all sorts of sounds. In addition to the frequent, unmistakable noises of their digestive systems, the animals command a broad and diverse range of grumbles, growls, and grunts by which they communicate with one another, individually and from group to group. Searching for food, the pachyderms must disperse over large areas, and in the dense bush they often lose sight of one another; but their grumbling and growling permit them to keep in touch acoustically even when they are more than a mile apart. They generate these eloquent sounds in their throats, while their trunks and their immense bodies act as a sounding board, amplifying the sounds and giving them their deep, hollow timbre. These sounds, or their absence, provide the basis for an efficient warning system: As soon as the animals sense any kind of danger, their growling abruptly stops. An eerie silence ensues. Suddenly, soundlessly, their trunks writhe skyward like S-shaped radars to read the air, and the animals stare mistrustfully in the direction of the suspect disturbance. Whether the cows will gradually resume their browsing and renew their "conversation" of grumbles, or whether—in case of serious threat—the herd will flee quietly on the soft soles of their feet, depends on the situation. Unless pandemonium breaks out and they crash through the brush in panic, elephants can leave an area almost inaudibly.

And they can *approach* just as inaudibly, as I discovered by accident. Hidden in the shrubbery of an embankment, I was watching a number of elephants squirting water at one another in a pit about two yards below me. I knew the spot well; it was the elephants' favorite water hole. I had taken up my hidden post before they appeared and had been waiting for them for about an hour. As they approached from the opposite direction, I felt sure that they hadn't noticed me. But the bush was so dense that only a part of the herd appeared in my viewfinder. While changing to a bigger lens, I obeyed a hunch and looked behind me. An elephant cow towered above the shrubs, head held high, staring down at me. She was only about three yards away. Not a sound had betrayed her arrival. The thrilling activities by the water forced me to disregard the cow; I shot many pictures before turning around once more, some twenty or thirty seconds later. The cow had disappeared as quietly as she had come. It must have been curiosity that had driven her to inspect my hiding place at close range.

At the edge of a small pool, the hollow pelvic bones of a dead elephant were bleaching in the sun. Other parts of the skeleton were scattered about. A family group with several young calves came strolling by. The mature animals trotted apathetically past the bones, but the smaller elephants were taken aback, warily sniffed the white hulk, and sidled uncomfortably past the remains of one of their own kind. In general, the carcasses of dead elephants seem to attract the living quite strongly. They examine the various pieces closely, seize some of the bones in their trunks, and carry them for hundreds of yards before dropping them again. Tusks seem to fascinate them in particular. Iain Douglas-Hamilton as well as Simon Trevor have taken films in which elephants extract the tusks of corpses, take them into their own mouths, and drag them over long distances.

A report by David Sheldrick, the late chief park warden of Tsavo National Park (East), confirms that this striking behavior on the part of elephants is by no means a random occurrence, but a characteristic—if seldom recorded—habit. Studies conducted in the Tsavo area for eight years show that a large number of tusks were found up to a half mile away from the corpses to which they belonged. Too heavy for hyenas, they could have been carried that far only by elephants. This behavior may well have contributed to the legend of elephant cemeteries.

Dense accumulations of bones tend to collect near places that are heavily frequented by the behemoths, such as water holes or bathing wallows. Old elephants are old mainly because their last set of molars is too worn for them properly to chew their food. For this reason, they prefer to stay in swampy areas where grass and plants are juicy and soft enough for chewing even with failing teeth. In the end, of course, they die there and their bones subsequently get spread around by other elephants. Wherever an especially large amount of bones happens to be strewn across a swampy meadow, it is easy to imagine a "cemetery." However, it is also possible that the accounts of elephant cemeteries passed on to us by hunters and adventurers are based on the remains of herds that perished together in some sort of catastrophe—perhaps a brush fire or a sudden eruption of gases—perhaps as a result of drinking poisoned water or of being killed in a large-scale battue hunt. Fantastic legends of elephant cemeteries have often captured our imagination, but such treasure troves of white gold exist only in adventure stories.

DISAPPEARING TRACES

Any of the observations I have made of elephants could as well have been made a hundred, a thousand, or even a hundred thousand years ago. It was during the Eocene epoch that a creature began proliferating all over Africa whose nose kept gradually growing into a trunk. During the late Miocene epoch, some five to fifteen million years ago, this "prototype" had already developed into the *Elephas primus*, ancestor of today's only two surviving elephant species—the *Loxodonta africana* (African elephant) and the *Elephas maximus*

(Indian elephant). Eventually, more than three hundred kinds of proboscidians —the zoological term for all animals equipped with a trunk—were to develop during the fifty-five million years since the pig-like *Moeritherium* made its first appearance. Most of them evolved over several million years and then died out because they could not adapt fast enough to ecological changes in climate or vegetation, or because faster-adapting species took away their food, dooming them to a process of starvation that lasted for hundreds of thousands of years. Only two species of the huge family of proboscidians, which once inhabited every region of the earth, have survived into the atomic age.

Among the fossilized footprints excavated in 1975 near Laetoli in Tanzania by anthropologist Dr. Mary Leakey are a few imprints of proboscidian giants. They were made by elephants of the species *Loxodonta exoptata*, and by a *Dinotherium*—a proboscidian whose tusks, contrary to those of present-day elephants, grew from the lower jaw and curved downward. The imprints contribute important circumstantial evidence of these creatures' existence and were left in a layer of volcanic flue ash which, under the influence of rain, solidified into tuff, thus preserving over the millennia a "foot-written" testimony of prehistoric life.

One fine prehistoric afternoon, the prairie must have been abuzz with heavy pedestrian traffic, for Mary Leakey's excavations have brought to light a number of traces left by an interesting variety of other animals, including those of two beings who walked erect. The parallel footprints of the two bipeds constitute the highlight among Leakey's finds. They are the mute chief witnesses of human genesis. With the help of carbon dating (potassium–argon dating), it has been established that they are 3.6 million years old. This find enabled Leakey to prove that at that time the first hominids were already walking erect on the long journey toward humanity—fully a half million years earlier than previous research had suggested. On that afternoon, two protohumans came walking through the prairie on two legs, free to use their hands. Some elephants and another proboscidian were nearby. And now, a few million years later, I stood in the same landscape, contemplating their discovered traces. Despite the afternoon heat, a chill ran down my spine: 3.6 million years was a hellishly long time, stretching into eternity as far as I was concerned. To me the prints of the hominids looked for all the world like those modern-day traces of people on the go that can be found on any sunny beach. As for the proboscidians, their memory lived on in the seals, almost round in shape, the largest measuring almost nine inches in length, pressed into petrified ashes.

The path from the scientists' camp to the excavation site led past a wallow. A recent thunderstorm had soaked the earth, and I noticed that the black mud clearly showed the plate-sized footprints of a present-day elephant. The ancient and fresh imprints were barely a few hundred yards apart! But the time that separated them seemed infinite.

Much has happened during the intervening millennia. What the first hominids' freedom to use their hands finally led to is common knowledge. At present, an increasing number of liberated hands are ready to push the atomic button in defense of world peace, a peace frequently defended by wars since antiquity. I recall Hannibal, who mobilized elephants to serve as his armies' armored corps and led them across the Alps. It didn't do the elephants much good.

Since the beginning of the Christian era, too many peace operations have combined with a thriving worldwide ivory trade to accelerate the decline of the North African pachyderms. As a military tool, elephants fast became obsolete, mainly because in the heat of battle they made no clear distinction between friend and foe. But as ivory producers, their popularity increased steadily. The need for ivory, one of the earliest items of international trade, killed off the elephants in North Africa; then, as supplies of white gold petered out, the slaughter of elephants spread south of the Sahara. For centuries, ivory was Africa's premier article of export, one that the tribes of the center of the continent could exchange for goods from the Orient. Long before the Portuguese, English, and other Christian seafarers discovered Africa on their expeditions in search of fame and riches, a lively white gold trade crossed the Indian Ocean from Africa to Arabia and Asia. But it took the advent of firearms for the ivory business to shift into highest gear. The Arabian merchants who had settled on Zanzibar and along the east coast of Africa began to ply their native "collaborators" with modern weapons. It became much easier to kill elephants, and the booming ivory trade provided a rationale for expanding the slave trade along the coast. In other words: Prisoners taken in brutal attacks on native villages were used to transport ivory reaped in equally brutal attacks on elephant herds. In long caravans, the victims of a greedy trade in human lives were driven from inside Africa to the coastal ports, usually carrying a double load—personal misfortune and heavy tusks— through the dust and heat of the African bush. It was a doubly lucrative business —for the Arabian merchants, at least!

Tippu Tib, a legendary slave trader of his time, once returned with twenty-seven tons of ivory from one of his safaris—safaris that averaged about ninety days of enforced marching from Uganda to the Indian Ocean. To judge by the weight of the booty, he needed more than a thousand slaves as carriers. With the colonization of Africa, white elephant hunters helped swell the ranks of the ivory suppliers. Statistics reveal the extent of the devastation: Toward the close of the nineteenth century, roughly eight hundred fifty tons of ivory were shipped to Europe each year. The most conservative estimates suggest that more than one million elephants were killed between 1830 and 1930.

For several hundred thousand years, the elephants had lived peacefully, undisturbed from generation to generation. But when they got caught in human history—especially in modern history—their fortunes drastically declined. South Africa, for instance, bragged a century ago of having "rid itself" of elephants. In the rest of Africa, the elephants' time has seemed to run out somewhat more slowly; but even so, their end is approaching with accelerating speed. Since the turn of the twentieth century, civilization and technology have been encroaching on all available space, even in Africa. Elephants are already crowded out of vast areas of their original territory, and their remaining habitat is severely threatened by the human population explosion.

According to a census taken in 1979 by the International Union for the Conservation of Nature (IUCN), Africa's elephant population stands at an estimated 1.3 million, minimum. The following table shows the distribution of the majority of these remaining elephants:

Angola	12,400
Kenya	65,000
Mozambique	54,800
Ruanda	128
Tanzania	316,300
Uganda	2,000
Zaire	377,700
Zambia	150,000

The data for this survey, the first of its kind, was gathered by a special task force, and it took three years to piece the puzzle together. The resulting statistics yield a wealth of information and include a head count of elephants in thirty-five African states. The elephant population seems to be stable in only seven of them. In all others, it is declining. Some countries show an abrupt decline; among these is Uganda, where an elephant population of 300,000 in 1973 had shrunk to only 2,000 by 1979. Concurrently conducted studies of the ivory trade suggest that from 50,000 to 150,000 elephants are being killed each year solely for their tusks. Since the killings are mostly the work of poachers, and the black market eludes statistical research, more precise figures are impossible to obtain. However, with ivory prices continuing to rise, the upper limit of 150,000 elephants slaughtered annually seems closer to the mark.

THE TRADE IN WHITE GOLD

A night soft as velvet covered the vast African bush. Mysterious bird calls pierced the silence from time to time. A hyena howled in the far distance. Somewhere, a few jackals barked shrilly at the moon, whose yellow light cast ghostly shadows across the landscape. Some giant figures emerged from the dark and slowly stepped out into a clearing. Others followed—several smaller shapes, then larger ones again. White sabers shone in the moonlight, gleaming against the dark silhouettes—ivory! Under cover of night, a herd of elephants had come out of the bush and was headed for the river to drink. Unhurried despite their thirst, the animals walked at a calm, measured pace along a well-worn elephant path that wound its way like a narrow road through the brambles.

The watering place was a broad, desolate strip of sand at the edge of the lazily rolling river. The animals came pushing through a sunken pass to the embankment. Suddenly shots rang through the night. Four massive figures collapsed. The dry cracking of a new round of shots mingled with the trumpet calls of the terrified behemoths. Panic seized the herd. But flight was difficult in the narrow hollow. The animals butted into one another, falling over and trampling their dying comrades to be felled by bullets in their turn. Only a few escaped, crashing madly through the undergrowth.

As soon as the noise died down, the poachers crept out of hiding. With axes and machetes, they cut the tusks from the dead elephants' jaws, taking only the ivory. Their filthy butchery kept them busy for the better part of the night. Then the leader gave a signal. A truck that had been waiting at a distance rolled up and the bloody tusks were loaded. A short while later, the engine started humming and the truck began to move; the poachers with their booty disappeared into the night. At last, the droning of the engine, too, faded away. Silence shrouded the dead. In the morning, vultures would be circling above the massacre, for some thirty elephants lay on the ground, including calves too young to bear tusks. Dead. Finished. Flies would soon swarm on the corpses.

Africa's friendly giants are defenseless against modern weapons, and in most of the continent's remaining elephant preserves they are frequently killed by organized poachers. In the past, the poachers were interested in the elephants' meat as well as their tusks, but ivory has become so valuable that they now are exclusively after the tusks—mountains of elephant flesh are left to rot. Certain gangs of poachers are equipped with semiautomatic weapons, usually taken from some military arsenal and readily available on the flourishing black markets. Other gangs go hunting with more traditional gear, such as poisoned arrows and snares. I once found a steel snare right in the middle of Manyara National Park, near the mouth of the Ndala River. A few weeks later, in the Selous area, I saw a bull with only half a trunk. To judge by the wound, he had lost the other half in a snare. In some regions, the killers use poisoned fruit or poison the water holes to kill elephants, or they trap smaller herds in carefully controlled prairie fires.

Rifle, poison, snare, or firetrap, the various instruments of the hunt are only a means to the same end—the tusks. During the 1970s, the price of ivory increased tenfold, from six to sixty dollars for every two pounds. In most of Africa's rural areas, sixty dollars is a small fortune. High prices for ivory, combined with the low standard of living in the hinterlands near the elephant preserves, have pushed poaching out of all proportion. This is borne out by the balance of trade. According to Kenya's official trade statistics for the year 1976, the nation exported fifty-five tons of ivory to Hong Kong; but according to Hong Kong's no-less-official trade statistics, Hong Kong imported two hundred thirty-five tons of ivory from Kenya. The difference between the two official versions clearly indicates the large quantities of illegally obtained ivory in international commerce. And the statistics are based on an average of a little more than twenty-two pounds of ivory for each elephant. This means that in 1976 Kenya sold to Hong Kong alone the ivory from 23,360 dead elephants. No wonder that between 1973 and 1977, Kenya's elephant population decreased by more than sixty percent—from 167,000 to 70,000. The statistics for Uganda are even more dismal. In 1966 about 8,000 elephants populated Murchison Falls National Park there. The park had attracted a large immigration of elephants, and to reduce the overpopulation the administration launched a shooting program. Ten years later, only 1,700 animals were left. Poachers and soldiers of Idi Amin's army had corrected the situation after their own fashion. In 1980, after Uganda's war with Tanzania, researchers could count only 160 elephants in the same area.

Some governments actively protect their country's wildlife—and this of course includes their elephants. Others do nothing. Speaking for many African nations, President Julius Nyerere of Tanzania formulated his government's commitment to the protection and preservation of African wildlife in his Arusha Manifesto of 1961:

> The survival of Africa's animal world is for all of us a matter of great significance. These creatures [and] the wilderness they inhabit are not only an important source of wonder and inspiration, but are also an integral part of our natural resources, of our future livelihood, and of our well-being.
>
> By holding our animal world in trust, we solemnly declare that we shall do everything within our power to ensure that our children and grandchildren, too, will be able to enjoy this rich and precious heritage.
>
> The preservation of wild animals and their environment calls for specialized knowledge, skilled workers, and financial support, and we urge other nations to share with us in this important task whose success or failure will affect not only the African continent, but the entire rest of the world.

Unfortunately, the years since then have shown all too often that good intentions are not always followed by good deeds. Idi Amin allowed soldiers of his army to go elephant-hunting with machine guns. In the Central African Republic "Emperor" Bokassa, before his fall, was a partner in a company that made enormous profits by selling his country's ivory harvest abroad. Guerrillas in Angola, Mozambique, and Ethiopia have decimated their elephant populations and traded the ivory off for weapons.

The survey of the African elephant conducted by the IUCN has revealed that many a politician's interest in his country's elephants is directly proportional to the credit received by his Swiss bank account for dollar-heavy tusks. In 1976 Zaire joined the Convention on International Trade in Endangered Species of Wild Fauna and Flora (CITES); in addition, it issued a ban on all hunting. But this step, which appears to be so commendable, seems to have been the prelude to a slaughtering of gigantic proportions. Several tens of thousands of elephants were killed in 1978. The magnanimous authorities granted export licenses for 1,000 (!) tons of ivory "produce," which could then be legally exported. When the president learned of the massacre, he ordered the exports stopped. But large quantities of ivory continued to leave the country. There are several interesting points to this story: First, the export licenses were granted to firms owned by an influential member of the politburo; second, a private C-13, a four-engine freight plane, was used to smuggle monthly deliveries of ivory to Johannesburg; third, bringing the merchandise to South Africa meant dealing with black Africa's political archenemy; and fourth, two member nations of the CITES convention had thus violated the convention's regulations. Business is business, even in Africa. Almost all states have well-formulated animal protection and hunting laws designed to prevent a ruinous exploitation of national treasures. But the governments of few countries actually enforce these laws. Furthermore, corruption and disinterest are rampant among the poorly paid officials of many states, so that on a bill of lading a shipment of tusks can easily turn into a load of teakwood.

Hong Kong, China, or Japan welcome as much raw ivory as they can get, and turn it into high-priced finished goods such as decorative carvings, jewelry, billiard balls, and the like. The finished products travel again halfway around the globe to the metropolises of Europe and the United States, where they end in the exclusive boutiques frequented by the rich. Especially since the oil crisis, the ivory market has been booming. Record quantities of white gold sell at record prices. In recent years, it has become evident that, as a hedge against inflation, people in business are investing in ivory, a durable and precious material in necessarily dwindling supply. Like gold, though of course on a smaller scale, white gold is becoming "hard currency" and an object of speculation. And now, wanting to remain in a lucrative business, poachers bring ever-smaller tusks to the black market; in other words, younger and younger elephants are sacrificed to the international ivory boom.

Some governments and park administrations do what they can to stop the illegal sellout of elephants at the hands of poachers. Wildlife patrols and gangs of poachers often wage battles, and many a ranger pays with his life for his courageous stand against the gangsters—who are usually better armed. For financial reasons the patrols are often insufficiently equipped. But even if park authorities and governments could afford the best weapons and equipment, they couldn't hope to win the guerrilla war for ivory, for in the long run the lure of high profits is too irresistible for the poachers and, too, both the businesses that back them and the countryside where the gangs operate are too vast and difficult to survey.

"Poaching must be stopped!" For decades this demand has figured in the programs of many African governments. Nevertheless, to date, poaching has proved impossible to stop. On the contrary, in recent years poaching has steadily increased, even in areas patrolled with small aircraft and helicopters. It seems very difficult, if not impossible, for any one nation acting on its own to check or completely prevent poaching. It remains to be seen whether an international convention—for instance, a trade agreement of some sort among the principal consumer countries—can help achieve the goal. In 1977 the African elephant was put on Appendix II of the CITES agreement, which has been signed by more than forty member states, including the major ivory-importing states—Hong Kong, the United States, and West Germany. The convention rules that member states will henceforth import only ivory that has been obtained legally. At best, then, most of the worldwide ivory trade would in the future involve legal merchandise only and consequently would be easier to control and direct. It is too early to tell whether this regulation can really be put into practice, and whether it could actually dry up the black market in ivory. For it is easy to lie on paper, especially on export documents covering ivory shipments. A shortage resulting from restricting the legal ivory supply could all too easily push black market prices for white gold even higher.

TOO BIG, TOO MANY, TOO HUNGRY

The loss of space in which to live and move about has created yet another "elephant problem" for some of the national parks and wildlife preserves. Elephants—always depicted as uncommonly clever animals in legends and fairy tales—seem to distinguish clearly between hunting areas and wildlife preserves. They therefore flee from the pressure of poachers and settlers to the wildlife preserves, where the influx can cause localized pockets of overpopulation that have devastating effects on the ecology. To be sure, elephants have been capable also of totally ruining a forest in a matter of years or, from the biologist's perspective, of turning it into grassland. Their wasteful, carefree eating habits are not recently acquired. Formerly, however, they could migrate freely, abandoning a depleted area and allowing it to reforest before they returned, at times after several decades. At present, the amount of room allotted to them in many countries is reduced to separate islands of refuge amid an ocean of human settlements and farmland. Elephants are no longer able simply to abandon an area that has suffered extensive damage from their profligate life-style and that urgently needs to be regenerated. In some cases, the stock of trees and brush has been so thoroughly worked over by the elephants that whole landscapes offer nothing but desolate fields of stunted growth.

Many scientists and wildlife managers are greatly upset by this destruction, and they accuse the elephants of drastically altering the balance of nature. Upon the recommendations of these authorities, thousands of elephants have been officially condemned to death. Some national parks even run their own slaughterhouses. In South Africa's Kruger National Park a fixed quota of elephants are being shot annually and turned into steaks to forestall an undesirable increase in the herd's population. And in Zambia's Luangwa Valley, as well as in the Wankie National Park of Zimbabwe, elephant butchers set to work every year during the dry season.

"Cropping" is the clever euphemism for this modern form of game husbandry. The croppers' work is made easy by the strong team spirit that within each family group characterizes elephants' social behavior. Threatened with danger, an elephant group huddles tightly together, taking calves and adolescent animals into their midst. The rangers, equipped with army guns, shoot the large cows first. Instead of fleeing, the other animals press around the victims in helpless confusion and in search of protection, unwilling to abandon their dying companions. Then they, themselves, get shot. Elimination of an entire family group in a very short time is a simple chore. The wildlife management of Kruger National Park has carried the technique one step further: Its "cropping" missions are run by helicopter.

The method of annihilating entire families rather than specific animals—say, mature bulls who are the most destructive to vegetation—is in line with the park administration's concept of efficiency. First, the administration is reluctant to disrupt the strong personal relationships that exist among the individual members of an elephant family. Second, selective massacre within a group would tend to encourage aggressively destructive behavior in the survivors. Third, it is safest not to leave witnesses: Croppers intent on carrying out their ecology-inspired operations don't want news of the slaughter to be transmitted to other elephant groups, who, fearing a similar fate, might prematurely flee.

Is the butchery necessary? Is it necessary to deny the elephants' right to life on the basis of forecasts of an ecological doomsday? Is there no solution to the dilemma of the elephants, who, driven from the last few spaces in the wild by the poisoned arrows and guns of the poachers and by encroaching settlers, must flee to the national parks and preserves that have been established for the express purpose of protecting endangered species—only to make themselves unwelcome? Who determines how many elephants an ecosystem or national park can support? Who dares decide that the toppling of trees threatens the balance of nature, which must be defended with machine-gun fire and cyanide capsules? The kind of balance that, in the opinion of certain scientists and park managers, is being upset by the elephants is not a divinely ordained order to be gleaned from the annual rings of toppled trees. It is merely a concept of order which people impose on nature as though they were infallible, and which they expect elephants to respect. For the adherents to this static concept of balance, it is imperative to protect the status quo from disturbance of any kind, including the felling of trees. But nature's equations of life and death treat elephants and trees as variables; nature does not submit to rigid rules and regulations. The dynamic balance of nature can, if at all, only be described as the irregularly oscillating result of multiple, ever-changing, interconnected processes.

What happens when an elephant destroys an acacia? Most of the biological energy stored in the tree will remain within the ecological system, even while it is being processed—for instance, when the elephant, in digesting it, turns it into fuel. The rest decomposes and is absorbed into other organisms, where it serves as raw material for new growth. As far as the ecology—energy budget is concerned, the toppling of a tree doesn't "destroy" anything; it merely modifies the habitat. Woodland turns into grassland for a prolonged period, but the process is not irreversible. Under favorable climatic conditions such as regular, long rainy seasons, the process works just as well in reverse: Prairie can soon be studded with bushes and trees.

Tsavo National Park in Kenya offers a classic example of the so-called elephant problem. In the 1960s, the park had a population of 20,000 elephants; as many as 40,000 elephants were living within an ecosystem that extended far beyond the park's boundaries. Slowly but surely, woodland and bush turned into grassland. In the opinion of many people, this change constituted destruction. They demanded that steps be taken to rectify it. The government decided in 1965 to reduce the elephant population by shooting 5,000 animals, but the decision caused a public outcry and was revoked the following year. From 1970 to 1972 a severe drought claimed the lives of 6,000 elephants. At the same time, poachers became more active. By 1975, poaching had reached formerly unheard-of proportions. Its toll for the Tsavo region amounted to 26,000 victims in merely five years, and energetic steps had to be taken for the elephants' protection. Today the ecosystem of Tsavo has only 10,000 elephants instead of the 40,000 animals that previously lived there. The scientists who once had advocated massive shooting programs had not taken enough factors into their zoological accounts. Above all, their complex computations involving the rate of tree loss, density variations, birth and death rates, and intervals between pregnancies had failed to account for the effects of poaching. Economic interests had made a shambles of ecological prognoses.

The massive number of elephant deaths during drought years offers a compelling example of nature's own—in this instance, catastrophic—method of population control. The victims, because of the elephants' social system, were almost exclusively cows and calves. As a result, the elephants were not only reduced in numbers, but their entire reproductive potential was compromised. The composition of their population had shifted dramatically, inevitably causing a disproportionate decrease in the reproduction rate for many years. It is safe to assume that similar, irregularly occurring natural catastrophes have always regulated the elephant population, so that its numbers increased and decreased in long swings of the pendulum from drought to drought, depending on the interrelated conditions of climate and available food. In addition, elephants have their own specific kind of birth control: The English zoologist Richard Laws conducted studies in Uganda and found that the average interval between a cow's pregnancies lengthened from four to nine years when feeding conditions deteriorated; simultaneously, the age at which a young cow reached reproductive maturity was delayed from twelve to eighteen years. This leaves no doubt that elephants react to environmental changes, including those of which they themselves are partly the cause. But as their life cycles are long, it may take years before their reactions begin to take effect.

The severity of the elephant problem varies according to local conditions. In southern Tanzania's Selous region, it is negligible, notwithstanding an elephant population of 110,000 animals. In the Tsavo area, it has

89

been solved by drought and poaching. In Serengeti National Park, authorities are allowing the herds to regulate their own numbers. In Uganda, the problem disappeared with the elephants. In Zambia, Zimbabwe, and South Africa, park managers use armed force to make the elephant population conform to their theories of nature's balance. The elephant problem has split nature conservationists into two opposing factions. One side sees it as a culturally induced problem that nature cannot be trusted to solve with obsolete methods that move at an excruciatingly slow pace. The other side warns us not to meddle too much with nature and to be wary of short-term studies or studies that take only ecological data into account while overlooking politico-economic developments such as militant unrest or poaching. But whatever the ecological arguments—for instance, that population reduction by shooting might accelerate birth rates—many people simply find repugnant the idea of mass killings of defenseless animals in national parks.

AFRICA 2000— TOO SMALL FOR GIANTS?

In Africa, as elsewhere, improved living conditions due to medical and technological progress have resulted in an abrupt increase in population. For decades, the waves of an intense human population explosion have spread quietly, but unchecked, across the entire continent, and are still spreading. Increasing between two and four percent annually, a country's population can double in less than twenty years. Kenya's government and economy, for example, must cope with a yearly population increase of roughly four percent. At that rate, it takes less than seventeen years for the population to double. Kenya had about 13 million inhabitants in 1974; it will have 34 million by the year 2000, in the view of experts. This dramatic development may also be seen in

Zimbabwe. In 1900, only a half million people were living in that region, formerly known as Rhodesia. But statistical forecasts anticipate 14 million inhabitants by the year 2000, fully twenty-eight times as many as at the beginning of this century. According to a forecast for the entire continent, contained in the American report "Global 2000," Africa's 399 million inhabitants of 1975 will have increased to 814 million people by the first year of the next century. They all must be fed, so that more and more land is being converted to agriculture; herds of cattle are advancing and taking over the last, barely serviceable grazing grounds.

During the twentieth century, Africa's wilderness, which, since Livingstone and Stanley's time, excited Europeans and Americans alike, has come under the plow and been divided and subdivided, leaving little room for elephants and other wild animals. The pachyderms' ancestral lands, which, except for desert areas, once encompassed all Africa, are now producing corn and bananas, millet and cotton, and other such plants needed to feed a relentlessly growing population; or they have become pastures for cattle. A study published in 1962 by Brooks and Buss, two British scientists, revealed that in 1929 seventy percent of Uganda was elephant habitat. By 1959 this had shrunk to seventeen percent. By 1999 only one or two percent, at best, will remain for the giants.

Experts believe that areas with a population density in excess of three inhabitants per square mile leave no room for elephants. The population density of many regions of Africa already exceeds this figure, or will reach it within the next decades. Faced with this pressure, elephants flee into the national parks and wildlife preserves, which at most amount to only two or three percent of their former territory; and by the year 2000, elephants will scarcely be found anywhere else on the continent.

It would, too, be utterly optimistic to take for granted that these parks and preserves can continue to exist at their present size. Many of them have been in existence for forty, fifty, or sixty years. They were established at a time of sparse population, when virgin land existed in abundance. Some preserves, in fact, were established in regions of so little rainfall and such poor soil that there was no other alternative for putting the land to good use. This situation has changed radically and will continue to change. The rapid population increase and the competitiveness that comes with it will force the people to find ways to subsist even in areas formerly thought uninhabitable. Thanks to modern technology, poor soil and meager rainfall are no longer insurmountable obstacles to the spreading of human settlements. Already, increased exploitation of the lands surrounding parks and preserves presses in on their boundaries. In many cases, it is highly doubtful that governments will be able and willing to maintain their national parks and nature preserves at their present size until the year 2000 and beyond in the face of these mounting pressures. The subject is political dynamite. Nature preserves may indeed be transformed into new settlements and agricultural acreage. And, of course, Africa's unchecked human population explosion is fraught with the dangers of aggravating social conflict and international tension. Uganda is a good example of the devastation that political unrest and war can inflict on national parks.

Caught between the loss of their habitat and the ivory boom, elephants face a bleak future indeed. The wilderness in which they developed, and for which evolution during the course of many thousands of years equipped them with appropriate tools and behavior, has, except for a few small enclaves, long ago disappeared. And here they are, the pachyderms, with their

92

gigantic bodies and gigantic appetites, confronted by a world where only dwarfs have a slim chance of survival. The shooting programs instituted in many parks are a bitter reminder that true wilderness, in which nature can successfully maintain its own balance over seemingly infinite eons of time, no longer exists. Such programs reduce the parks to merely big open-air museums where a carefully computed number of elephants are allowed to display themselves as living curiosities.

Some people spend all their time and energy trying to secure a niche for the elephants, a hiding place, a few asylums where they can survive into the twenty-first century, these friendly giants who cut such dignified, yet pathetically forlorn, figures as they straggle into modern times. Meanwhile, many other people spend at least as much time and energy extracting as many elephant tusks as possible for personal gain. Ivory prices will probably continue to rise more drastically than those of any other raw material, making the last few elephant herds an increasingly profitable target for hunters. Any bull who walks around Tanzania with a healthy pair of tusks walks around with five times as much money in his mouth as a Tanzanian farmhand can earn in one year; and by the end of this millennium, the elephant's tusks may well be worth ten times as much. If the farmhand is caught poaching, he gets a few months of jail. Therefore, if he exchanges his hoe for a gun or poisoned arrow, he takes a gamble that, for a poor man, is well worth the risk. And Tanzania's population will soon have twice as many poor men—not to mention their hungry wives and children—as it has today. Large elephant herds living in the wild can survive into the twenty-first century only if the governments of the countries in which they live take drastic measures for their protection and can muster enough popular support to enforce these measures. In most cases, however, the cost involved will prove prohibitive for the strained budgets of developing nations.

Elephants, with the rest of Africa's wildlife, constitute a unique heritage for all of us. Even the people of rich industrial nations have a moral claim to it. But anyone who lays a moral claim to such a heritage should at the very least be willing to help pay to preserve it. The developing countries can hardly be expected to defray the cost of a worldwide heritage for the chief benefit of tourists from affluent industrial nations. Most inhabitants of black Africa cannot afford a single visit to one of their parks. These "national" parks should become "international" parks, at least where their financial support is concerned. They have long been international in their attendance. Many ecology-oriented organizations—IUCN, World Wildlife Federation, or the Zoologische Gesellschaft Frankfurt, to name a few—have for years made great efforts to support the national parks and to make many of their programs possible. If some public funds from the ecology budgets of technologically advanced countries were made available, the various separate aid efforts could perhaps be consolidated to form a network of sponsorship for Africa's national parks. In addition to general operating funds, technical and administrative expertise, where needed, would also have to be made available by the sponsors and to be accepted by the African partners. At present, ecologists and wildlife managers of some national parks are still at odds about the best strategy to solve the elephant problem: It is easier to protect the habitat from elephants, whose helpless trumpeting is no match for the suddenly trigger-happy wardens, than to protect elephants from the poachers.

While the two parties are busy arguing, professional ivory bandits are clandestinely ridding them of their problem. It happened in Kenya; it happened in Uganda. Will Africa's friendly giants cease to be today's problem and become tomorrow's legend?

COLOR PLATES

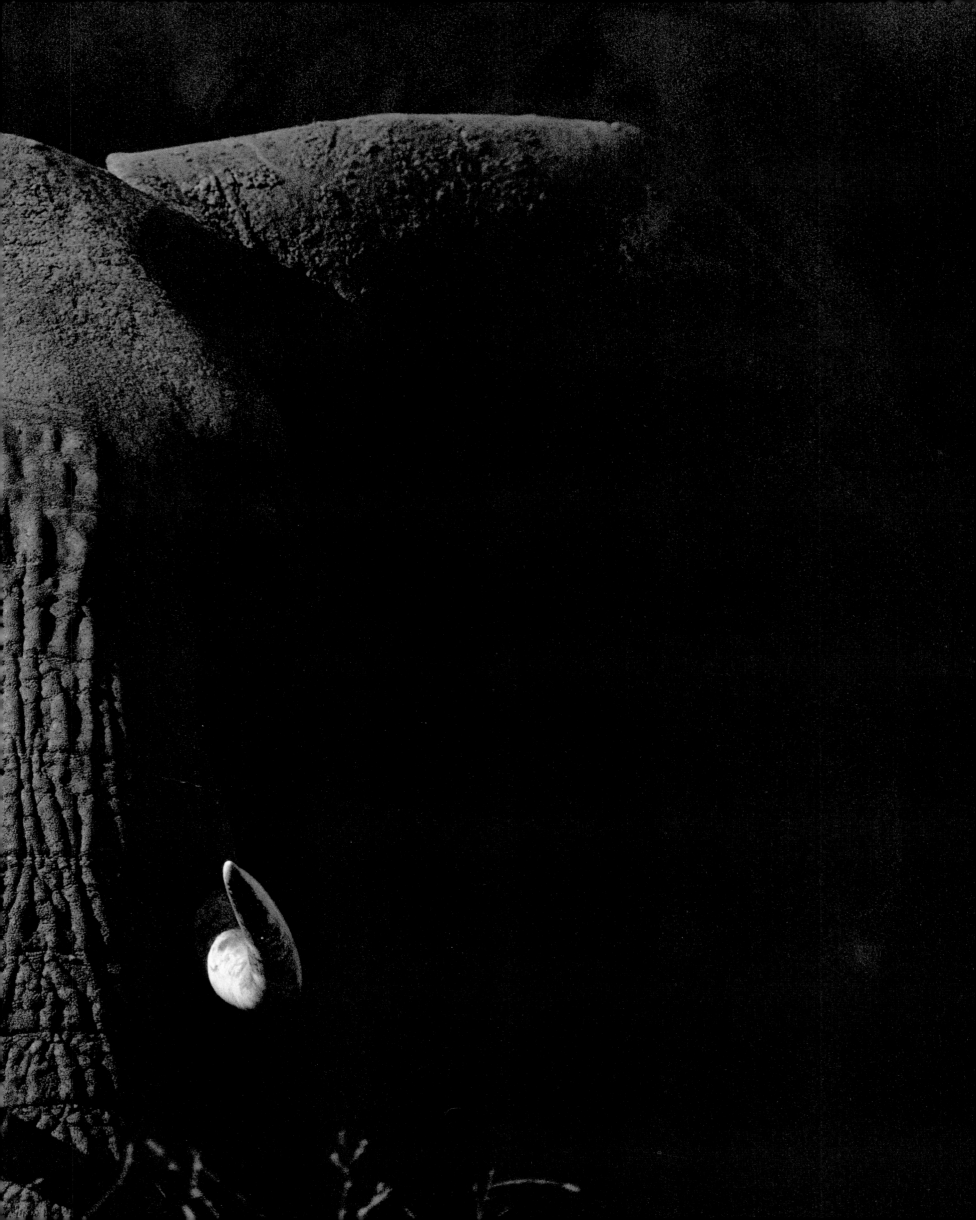

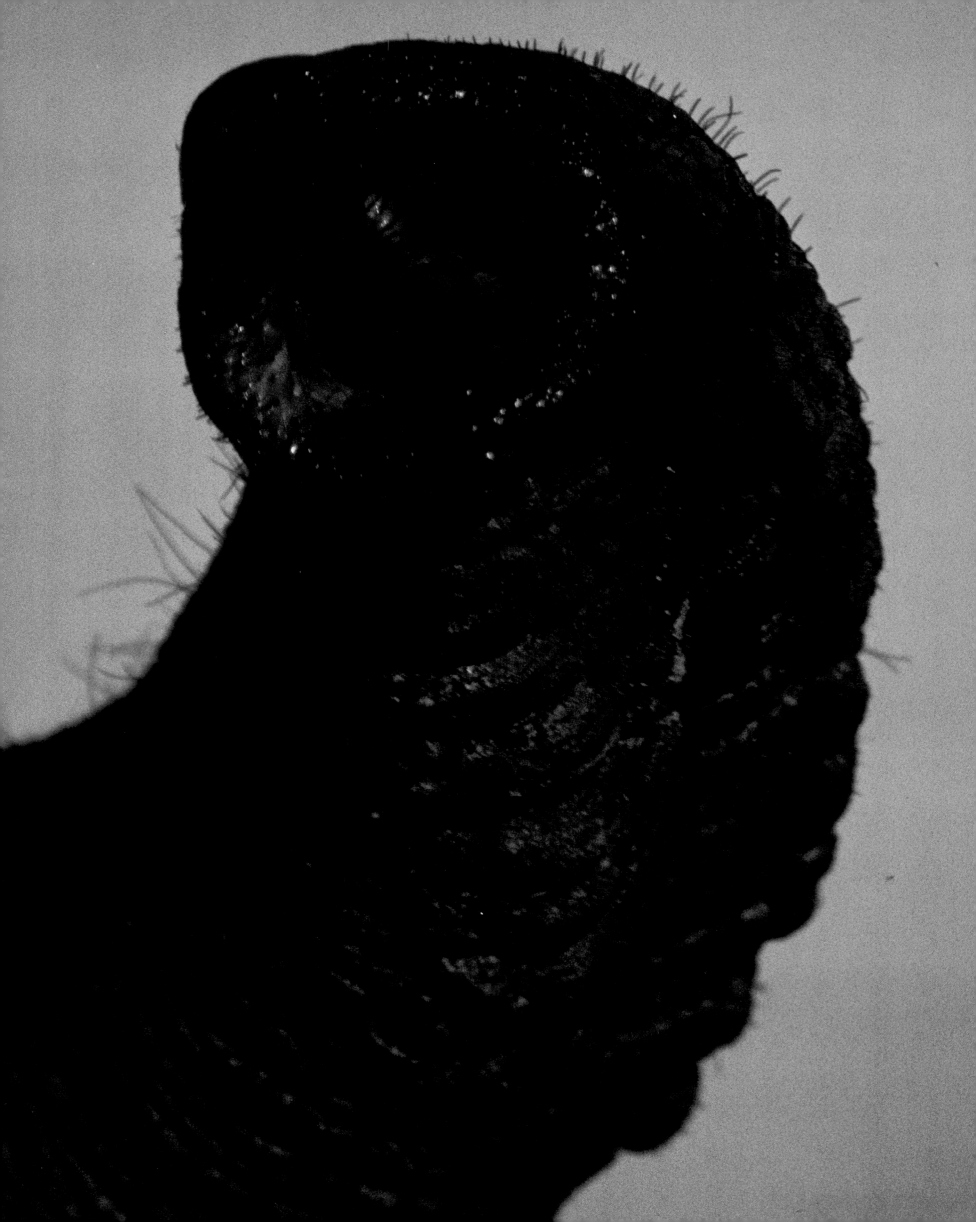

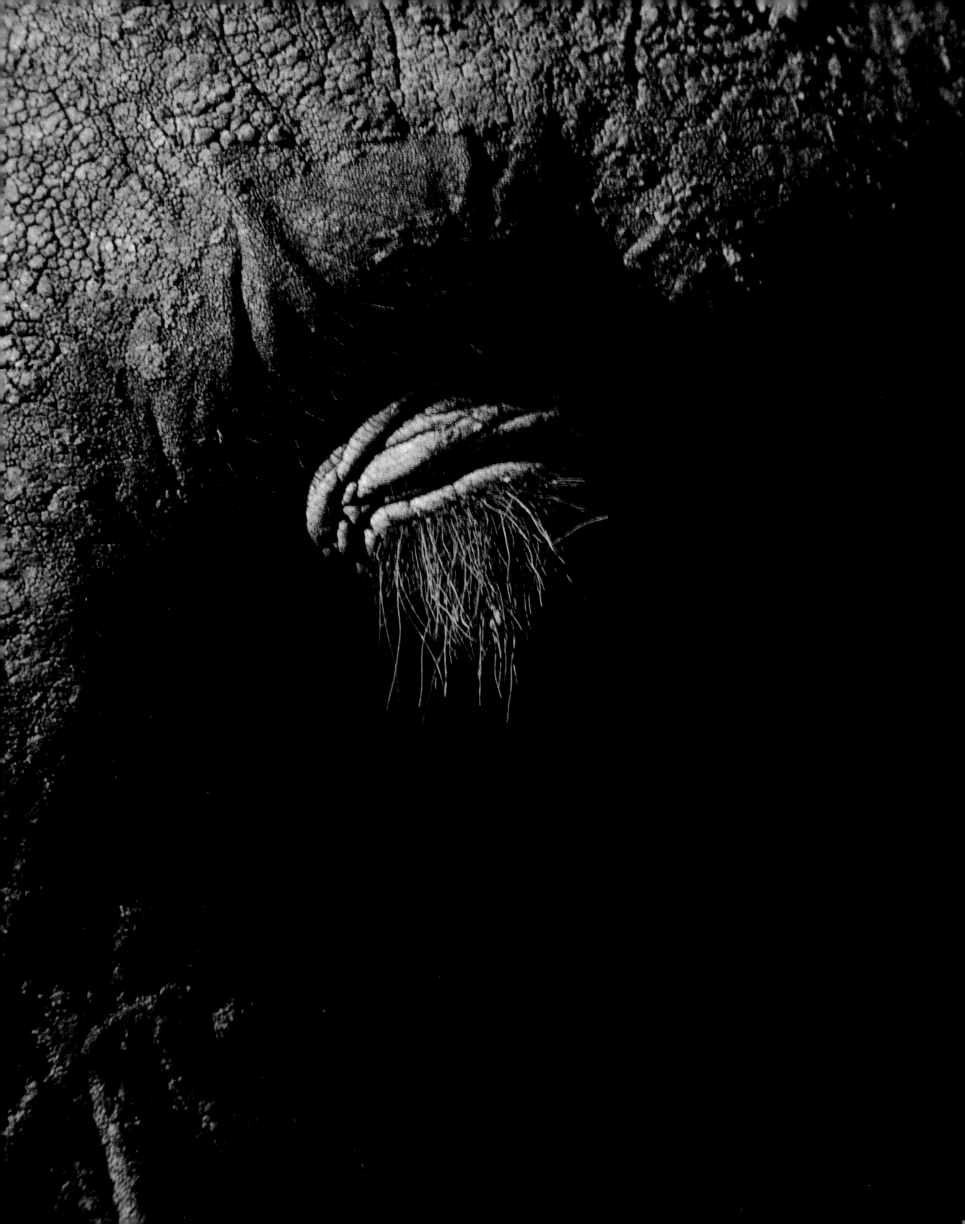

CAPTIONS TO THE COLOR PLATES

At sunrise, temperatures still are pleasantly cool. Elephants frequently choose this time of day to return from their nocturnal grazing grounds to the vicinity of watering holes.

Two bulls are crossing a branch of the Rufiji River. The oil palms in this area have been denuded by a storm.

Three elephants' trunks rise out of the water like the tentacles of giant octopuses. Pachyderms like to bathe frequently and can swim across deep rivers or lakes.

Thunderclouds are gathering behind some "big tuskers," members of a "club" of large bulls living in Tanzania's Ngorongoro Crater.

In Manyara National Park, trees of the species *Acacia tortilis* are the elephants' favorite food. The acacias in the background are in great jeopardy.

Left: This bull is reaching up into the branches of an umbrella acacia with his long trunk. Tall elephants are capable of defoliating treetops six or more yards aboveground.

Right: Having seized a few branch tips between the two fingers of his trunk, the elephant loops them around his nose muscle, then pulls the branch down.

A curious calf pokes his trunk at the observer. Because of poor eyesight, the elephant relies mainly on his sense of smell.

Top left: The bull takes the tree trunk between his tusks, lays his trunk full-length against it, grabs the fork of a branch to get a firmer hold, then leans against the tree with all his might . . .
Top right: . . . until the tree yields, groaning . . .
Bottom left: . . . slants lower and lower . . .
Bottom right: . . . and finally crashes to the ground.

Top left: This cow belongs to a group that spent one and a half hours under an acacia. In the end, the tree looked more like a weeping willow. Having eaten the bark of the branch, the cow proceeded to eat part of the soft wood itself.
Bottom left: Some scientists believe that the elephants' craving for the bark and branches of the *Acacia tortilis* stems from the particularly high calcium content of these trees.
Right: The elephants have peeled long strips of bark off the tree, leaving a deep wound from which the tree will not recover.

Left: The nearly circular sole of a large elephant's flat foot has a diameter of about twenty inches. Although the leathery skin is full of cracks, it seldom gets pierced by thorns.
Right: The prehensile fingers of an elephant trunk are so nimble that they can easily pluck a single blade of grass.

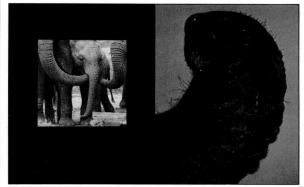

A calf plucks a few leaves from a thick tangle of branches. Elephants are very careless food gatherers, strolling from shrub to shrub, picking bunches of foliage here and there at random. Their failure to pick the shrubs clean allows the vegetation to recuperate in the long run.

This alert animal has sensed my presence and is reading the air in my direction. An elephant's ears can almost reach a length of one and a half yards. When spread, they are sensitive sound detectors as well as an efficient cooling system.

Left: The trunk plays an important part in providing body contact. Elephants often reach into each other's mouths; it is a form of greeting as well as a gesture of reassurance in moments of danger. Here, a mother and older sister happen to be simultaneously reaching for a calf's mouth.
Right: The tip of an elephant's trunk is really the tip of his nose, as the two nostrils show. The trunk ends in two prehensile appendages—a prerequisite for its surprising dexterity and versatility. The cross-ribbing ensures a firm grip.

In this wooded landscape shimmering in the sunset, the elephant does more than indicate scale. He represents the greatest danger to the forest, for he can, in time, transform these trees into a garden of sculptured remains.

Coiled up like a giant snake, the trunk rests on the tusk. At noontime, elephants like to doze in the shade, resting their trunks in all sorts of ingenious positions.

Elephants are so tall that they seldom lose their footing in rivers or lakes; yet they are perfectly capable of swimming considerable distances.

In protected areas, elephants stop to drink whenever they have an opportunity. But outside the national parks and wildlife preserves, they feel so threatened that they usually visit their watering holes only at night.

These bulls are spending the hot midday hours in the shallow waters along the shore of Lake Manyara. They obviously appreciate the cool water; but the soda content of the water makes it undrinkable.

Left: This bull considers me a nuisance and decides to attack.
Right: Ears spread menacingly, he comes charging. But it is a feint attack. Shortly before reaching me, he stops short.

This calf has not yet learned to use his trunk as a drinking hose. He therefore brings his mouth down to water level. He sticks out his hind leg to counterbalance this top-heavy position.

Top left: An adult elephant can fill his trunk with as much as ten quarts of water, which he then lets run down his gullet.
Top right: Serious confrontations among elephants are rare. These animals are perhaps simply fighting over a place in the water hole.
Bottom: An adult elephant drinks between 120 and 150 quarts of water each day. Under normal conditions, the animals quench their thirst at least once every twenty-four hours.

Top left: This young bull is splashing around strictly for fun. He uses his legs as well as his trunk to send sheets of mud into the air.
Top right: Calves do not have an innate knowledge of the many ways to use their trunks. It takes long training to learn how to manipulate the versatile nose muscles—for instance, by using the trunk as a drinking hose.
Bottom: These elephants cross the Rufiji River every morning and evening. During the day, they graze on the fresh swamp grass in the reed fields; at night, they search for food in the drier hinterlands.

Left: Three trunks are being lowered into a water hole the elephants had to dig into the sandy bottom of a dry riverbed. The competition for the precious liquid is fierce. While she is drinking, a mother cow will even block her calf's access to the water.
Right: The elephant throws his head back to empty his trunk to the last drop. He has to drink ten to twenty trunkfuls of water to quench his thirst.

Three calves are enjoying a companionable dust bath. They are perhaps four, three, and two years old.

An elephant's trunk is a combination of nose and upper lip. Activated by several thousand muscles, it is as versatile as a human arm.

Top left: A bull searching for salt attempts to dig up a termite hill.
Bottom left: Another elephant is loosening the mineral-rich earth of a salt lick to eat it. Elephants will sometimes march for miles to reach salt licks.
Top right: With a vigorous swing of her trunk, this cow covers herself with a load of dust. The "dusting powder" will help protect her skin from parasites.
Bottom right: When an elephant scrubs himself on the trunk of a tree or on a termite hill, it sounds as if his coat were being rubbed down with sandpaper.

In the sandy hollow of an embankment, three elephants are thoroughly showering one another with dust. The tassels on their tails are made up of long, thick hair.

The dust bath, along with the scrubbing and rubbing, is part of the elephants' daily hygiene.

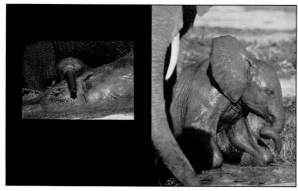

Left: Elephants usually are very friendly to and tolerant of one another. Bathing time, in particular, is a time for relaxation and games.

Right: The "knot" shows into what grotesque configurations an elephant can twist his flexible nose muscles.

A family enjoys its daily mud bath. The moist pap cools the elephants' skin and protects it against parasites.

This idyll is deceptive. The calf seems to be playing affectionately with his mother's tusk. In reality, his mother is brutally shoving him away from a watering hole in the sandy beach.

Left: This elephant cow is scratching herself between her forelegs with a stick that she is holding in her trunk as if she were holding a brush by its handle. Elephants are among the few animals capable of occasionally handling tools.

Right: The mud bath plays an important part in the elephants' daily hygiene, a time-consuming routine carried out with great care.

Being near a wallow incites these three calves to exuberant tomfoolery.

Top left: During the heat of the day, elephants move in slow motion. Toward evening, when temperatures begin to cool, the calves perk up. These two youngsters are playing tag.

Bottom left: The calves are testing their strength in playful combat.

Top right: One calf wantonly bites another's ear. The playful wrestling sometimes pitches very unequal partners against each other; but a difference in size doesn't matter.

Bottom right: These three calves are huddling in a sand pit, taking a break from their violent games.

Top left: Termite hills make ideal scrubbing stones to satisfy the elephants' urge to scratch.

Bottom left: Elephants take their time to "sandpaper" every inch of their skin.

Right: A calf cleans his ear with the tip of his trunk. Elephants sometimes rip out bundles of grass to use in cleaning their ear openings.

Elephant calves love close body contact. During a long siesta, a little calf climbed on top of another calf and remained there for several minutes before the calf on the bottom bothered to shake him off.

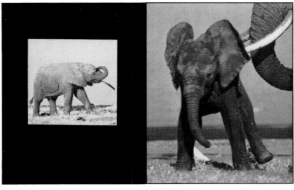

Left: The little bull flaunts a vulture feather that he had found on the ground. He carried it around for quite a while, first swinging it in his trunk, then sprouting it from his mouth. Getting bored, he finally dropped it.

Right: Swinging his trunk, this one-year-old runs to meet his playmates. Actually, elephants are unable to run or gallop. When attacking or in flight, they simply fall into a powerful trot.

Top left: This is one of the photos taken along the Rufiji River where it crosses the Selous Game Reserve. The elephants are on their way to a watering place, while the giraffes have already returned from the river.

Top right: The bulls, having just swum across the Rufiji River, are crossing a sandbank; they are heading for the reed fields in a swampy bog where they will graze for the rest of the day.

Bottom: I discovered this herd of more than one hundred elephants in the western part of the Serengeti.

The grass along the shores of Lake Manyara is especially nutritious. Elephants often browse here in the evening.

Left: This young elephant is feeding on tufts of grass that he grabs in his trunk, then pulls from the ground with a kick of his front foot.

Right: For several minutes, this young elephant was distracted by a stick that he found in his path. He finally dropped it to follow his mother, who had slowly moved on.

A family group crosses a shallow branch of the Rufiji River. The photograph was taken from a small airplane.

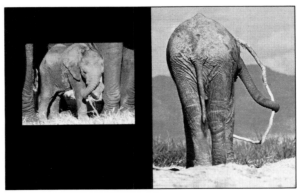

Left: Elephants love to play with an odd assortment of sticks and branches. Calves in particular test their dexterity by handling these "found objects."

Right: This adolescent looks like an archer as he handles a dry branch he found near a mud hole.

Top left: The elephant steps respectfully aside to make way for the flustered rhinoceros who has accidentally strayed into the elephant herd. Confrontations between the two species are extremely rare.

Bottom left: A young bull threatens one of the zebras who is passing by. On the whole, elephants are very tolerant of other species.

Top right: The unhurried stance of the elephant shows that he is unaware of the lion in the tree. Lions pose no threat to adult elephants.

Bottom right: Her resting place high up in the branches offers the lioness cool shade as well as a shelter from mosquitoes.

Many elephants must end like this. Poachers take their ivory tusks and leave the corpses to rot. In the foreground is the nerve that was lodged in the hollow upper third of one of the tusks.

This trunk is all that remains of a tree killed by elephants. It has become the sleeping place of crested cranes.

While a young lioness rips the intestines from the corpse of an elephant cow, the lioness herself was not the killer. The cow probably died of disease.

Elephants and these black rhinos share the same habitat; but the rhinos are several decades closer to extinction. At left, a cattle egret.

At dusk, impalas come stalking along the shore of Lake Manyara. But the water contains too much soda for them to drink it.

Left: This buffalo belongs to a herd of more than one hundred animals. The fruit he is chewing has stained his mouth red.

Right: Two zebra stallions are fighting for a mare. Lake Manyara is in the background.

Left: Two young elephants raise their probing trunks into the wind. Around water holes, elephants are particularly restive and quick to react to scents.

Right: This calf slides down a gentle slope on his bottom. Older elephants are less nimble and must find trees or termite hills with which to scratch their behinds.

The posture of quarreling calves already anticipates that of grown bulls fighting for rank. Although the youngsters can clash violently enough to break their tusks, serious injuries are extremely rare.

Elephants mate in less than a minute, but their gestation period lasts for twenty-two months.

Too young for tusks, and already fighting!

This oft-interrupted wrestling match took fully a half hour. The outcome of such combats often settles a dispute of prestige and seems to have a bearing on a bull's mating prospects. The bull on the right won the match and was seen mating two days later.

Top: A herd in flight. It was not possible to determine what routed them; perhaps they sensed the presence of lions, or perhaps some noise frightened them.

Bottom: Elephants on the go. Shuttling back and forth between water hole and grazing grounds, elephants sometimes march twenty miles each day.

Left: Elephant calves display prepubescent sexuality at a tender age.

Top right: A bull discovers a cow ready to mate . . .

Bottom right: . . . and pursues her impetuously for some hundred yards.

Left: A very young calf pushes his way between the legs of his mother and elder sister. Older animals in a family give wide berth to the antics of youngsters.

Top right: Sharing a shower! As part of her daily bath, this cow squirts water on her back, flanks, and belly with broad swings of her trunk. Her little calf, only a few months old, gets thoroughly soaked in the process.

Bottom right: During the first weeks of life, a baby elephant perceives little of the world around him. He rarely strays more than a few yards from his mother's pillar-like legs.

The trunk plays a major part in ensuring close contact between mother and child. This cow is not only guiding her young calf around an obstacle in their path, but is also soothing him with her touch.

Left: The head of the baby giraffe being born looks almost black. The birth took almost three quarters of an hour; finally, the baby fell about two yards to the ground.

Right: At first, the newborn could barely lift its head, but it rallied quickly. About an hour later, it was standing on its own legs.

Left: Even a newborn calf drinks ten quarts of milk each day. Unlike the mammaries of most other mammals, those of elephant cows are between the forelegs.

Right: A suckling calf leans his trunk on the mother's belly or lets it swing freely overhead. Calves begin to be weaned when they are two or two and a half years old; but some cows are willing to nurse even seven- and eight-year-olds.

Top: This family group passes several dead trees on its way to nocturnal grazing grounds. These particular trees perished in a flood; elephants didn't destroy them. Lake Manyara is in the background.

Bottom left: Despite a relatively high probability rate of 1:100, twin births among elephants have been observed only in very rare instances. These two suckling calves are probably twins.

Bottom right: At first the cow tried to chase one of the calves away with a kick and an angry growl; but in the end she allowed him to drink. The calves are two to two and a half years old.

Here, elephants are trotting two by two along car tracks in Manyara National Park. Their own footpaths are only sixteen to twenty inches across—wide enough for only single-lane traffic.

Top left: Elephants can outrun humans. But they heat up quickly and after a short run at top speed must slow their pace.

Top right: Taken against the light, this photograph clearly shows the long, prickly hair of the calf. Newborn elephants are bluish-black in color and covered with a reddish fuzz.

Bottom: In late afternoon, the elephants retreat from the open plain to the acacia forest. The photo shows only part of a herd, made up of fifty or more animals gathered from several families.

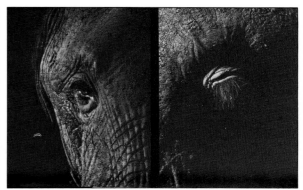

Top left: Three calves cuddle up during play.

Bottom left: This calf is sleeping under his mother's belly during the hot midday hours. Adult animals don't lie down at noontime, but will lie down to sleep for a few hours after midnight.

Top right: The calf tries stubbornly to pull a piece of bark from his mother's mouth. The tips of his growing tusks are already pushing out from under their skin folds.

Bottom right: A calf touches the corner of an older sister's mouth. Reaching into another elephant's mouth not only teaches young elephants what plants belong on their daily menu, but the contact also reassures and comforts them.

Left: Two cows help a calf over the slippery edge of a mud hole.

Right: This pachyderm is blaring his exuberance abroad.

Left: The bull's eye glistens in the slanting light.

Right: An elephant's eyes appear very small compared to the size of his body. Long lashes on the lid protect the eyeball.

The first rain has been long in coming. The animals now greedily suck up the fresh water.

At a leisurely pace, the elephants are trekking to their nocturnal grazing grounds on the mountain slopes. An insatiable stork accompanies the herd.

Elephant bulls often form little "clubs"; but in a solitary mood, they can also spend days roaming the countryside all by themselves. Towering clouds herald the rainy season.

The lead cow catches the last rays of the setting sun. The slanting light accentuates the network pattern of her wrinkled skin.

Sunset. Against the slope of a mountain, the silhouette of a baobab. Fond of the soft wood that they pry loose with their tusks, elephants can dig veritable caves into the trunks of these giant trees.

A full moon is rising in the east while the sun sets in the west. Their light was just enough to take a few pictures of this evening scene.

An uncommonly fine pair of tusks adorns this cow. The tusks of females often crisscross, which doesn't inconvenience them in the least. The tusks of bulls, on the other hand, tend to curve outward.

PHOTOGRAPHIC TECHNIQUE AND WORKING METHOD

Photographing elephants was simple, I thought at first. The animals were big and therefore easy to find; they weren't particularly shy and usually they traipsed leisurely through the countryside. Hence there was not even danger of blurring the picture.... Then I began to photograph elephants. About ten thousand pictures later, I had changed my opinion considerably. The pachyderms are such endearing, interesting creatures that stalking them is a fresh pleasure each day. But beyond showing what elephants look like, the photographer must capture something of the dignity, composure, strength, playfulness, and worldly wisdom that are the essence of the animal.

The more I watched them, the more I wanted to translate my experience into pictures. My respect and admiration for these mighty but friendly giants made my self-appointed task weigh heavily on me. I urgently wanted to show them in the acacia forest at dawn ... enjoying their bath at noontime ... engaging in combat in the evening. But compressing three-dimensional moments into two-dimensional pictures without losing much of the spice is difficult. It even imposes technical restrictions: I like to work with my camera's motor drive on; it allows me to keep my eye on the viewfinder and concentrate entirely on the image. But the elephants, upset by the faint humming of the motor, would turn tail on me and bolt out of range. After several attempts, I finally had to remove the motor from my camera and leave it back in the hut.

To give myself as broad a range as possible, I had dismantled the windows and window frames on both sides of my car. In some instances this worked to my disadvantage, for elephants possess an excellent sense of smell. Sometimes when I positioned myself, I paid attention solely to the direction of the light, without simultaneously heeding the wind. The pachyderms unexpectedly turned up their noses and, picking up my scent, turned on their heels and made off on their soft soles. Certain herds, on the other hand, quickly got used to the Land-Rover in which I pursued them for days; some elephants, searching for food, came within reach of the car and sniffed it, intrigued. Other groups never overcame their initial shyness, making it impossible for me to draw close enough to photograph them. It took about fourteen days before the "wild" bulls near lakes Ndutu and Masak allowed me to follow them at close range, enabling me to photograph them toppling a tree. I finally dared to accompany them on a swim. Oddly enough, elephants and other animals in the wild can tolerate a big, noisy Land-Rover moving at close range, but a distant pedestrian can put them to flight or prompt them to attack. As I could hardly risk disrupting my work every ten minutes to run for cover because of an angry bull, most of the photographs in this book were taken from my car and only a few were made on foot or from the water.

My photographic equipment consisted of two Leicaflex cameras and one Leica. All three took quite a beating. No matter how hastily I changed films, some sand, dust, or saltwater always sneaked in. Tropical rains hosed the cameras down like cars in a car wash. Once, when my brakes failed, the car shot down a steep slope, severely testing the cameras' indestructibility in the fall. But my cameras never failed me—a remarkable feat, given the conditions of the African bush. Dented and battered, they simply underwent a certain external restyling.

Most of the time, I chose long focal lengths, using the Elmarit-R 1:2.8/180 mm, the Telyt-R 1:6.8/400 mm, and the Telyt-R 1:6.8/560 mm. But I also had occasion to use the Summicron 1:2/90 mm, the Elmarit-R 1:2.8/35 mm, and even the Super-Angulon 1:4/21 mm.

When measuring light, especially when long focal lengths made spot-metering necessary, I discovered that the elephants' dark skin consistently fooled my meters with incorrect values. Although I had calibrated all three meters for normal light conditions and had carefully aligned them, they consistently indicated only half the proper light value when directed at distant elephants within range of the telephoto lens. I constantly overtaxed the lenses by one full F-stop, at times even by one and a half.

I used Kodachrome 64 and Ektachrome 400 films. These two kinds of film have become second nature to me over the years, so that in most situations I am able to judge the light values for them correctly and disregard the values indicated by my light meters. Both films generally come closest to my standards for color, sharpness, and contrast. How well they perform can be judged by the fact that some of the photos in this book have been enlarged thirty times (at a 1:30 scale).

Finally, I would like to mention one specific problem that, although not strictly a matter of technique, can nonetheless distinctly affect a photographer's skill—tsetse flies. These horsefly-like insects had a merciless way of stinging my hand at the precise moment when an elephant was captured in my viewfinder. The troublesome flies and I collaborated in producing quite a collection of blurred pictures, since, as I pushed the button, a tsetse fly would inevitably puncture my skin.